Cover:
Child with goose

Pages 2/3:
Altar sundial
The gathering of the twelve gods of Olympus symbolizes both the links that unite them and the distribution of their mutual power and functions, throughout the twelve months of the year.

Pages 6/7:
Five dancers before a door with Corinthian pillars
Known as the "Borghese Dancers".

Page 11:
The Kidnapping of Europa

Photographic credits:

R.M.N.: 1, 2/3, 6/7, 11, 13, 14/15, 17, 18/19, 21, 23, 25, 29,45, 50,51, 52/53, 55, 57, 59, 65, 66/67, 71, 73, 75, 77, 78/79, 82/83, 85, 87, 91, 92/93, 95, 96/97, 99, 100/101, 103, 107, 108/109, 111, 112/113, 116/117, 119,120.
Hervé Champollion: 38/39.
Philippe de Dreuille: 42/43, 46/47, 68/69.
Alain Mahuzier: 88/89.
Archives Tallandier: 80.
Dominique Repérant: 63.
Collection privée, D. R: 31, 33, 35, 37, 103/104, 121/123.
Text: Joël Schmidt
Contribution: F. B. S.B.

Published by Grange Books
an imprint of Grange Books Plc
The Grange
Kingsnorth Industrial Estate
Hoo, nr Rochester
Kent ME3 9ND
www.Grangebooks.co.uk
ISBN: 1-840136-898

ROMAN MYTHOLOGY

Joël Schmidt

Foreword
Pierre Brunel

Translated
by
Susan Taponier

Grange
BOOKS

FOREWORD

Here is a new, highly suggestive book offering a much-needed corrective. We have become so accustomed to associating Greek mythology with Roman mythology that we tend to confuse the two. Stéphane Mallarmé did just that in 1880 in his work *Les Dieux antiques*. He talked about "Greek and Roman, or classical, myths" that formed a "twofold mythology, Greek and Latin", in which "the Greek myths possess a value that Roman myths never acquired." He went so far as to say "Roman myths were almost always borrowed whole from the Greek Olympus, along with ready-made legends." In this book, Joël Schmidt has taken a completely different approach and rightly so. He has devoted a separate volume specifically to Roman mythology, which carries within its own reason for being.

This reason for being is quite simply Rome itself, a Rome more mythical for us than mythological, a Rome at once devouring and nourishing, admirably represented by the she-wolf. Rome indeed absorbed the best of Greece, and there has undoubtedly never been a dominant power that borrowed so much from the country it conquered. This is confirmed by the transition from Greek mythology to Roman mythology. The name of Apollo designated in both languages and both religions the god of light, who could also be an enigmatic, cruel god. For Mallarmé, Apollo was not a Roman god. Yet, in Rome, he was joined to the figure of Lucessius, the old Oscan name for Jupiter. Similarly, the figure of Pluto was not an identical copy of Hades. In the *Inferno*, Dante still called him Dis, the name of an archaic divinity sprung from Italian soil, or rather from beneath the soil.

Though we often look for the gods in the sky, they are also found on the earth and in the earth. I am thinking here not only of Ceres, the goddess of harvest, or her daughter Proserpine, or Cybele, a complex divinity, less Hellenic than oriental, – the "Bérécynthienne" of Joachim du Bellay in *Roman Antiquities* (1558). Nothing is more revealing than the new episode concerning Hercules and Cakus, reflecting a local power struggle during the age of conquest.

Aeneas, the Trojan prince, was the leading figure in the primordial myth of the foundation of Rome. From the historian, Livy, we learned about Romulus and Remus, the twin boys fed by the she-wolf, but it took the genius of the poet Virgil to develop the epic adventures of Ulysses, the national hero, who succeeded in abandoning Dido in Carthage to fulfil his calling. Mythological figures were undoubtedly the pillars of the Roman pantheon, but the first task of Roman mythology was to shed light on and account for the foundation of Urbs, the ancient city of Rome.

Through the culture we have inherited, Jupiter, Juno, Mercury and Vesta have become as familiar to us as the streets of ancient Rome were to Montaigne. Yet we cannot help being captivated by the multitude of household gods, local agricultural gods and allegorical gods that give Roman mythology its special flavor, with whom the author has wisely chosen to begin this book. Among these so-called minor divinities, the one I would choose to remember is not Vertumnus, who represents change and metamorphosis, but rather Terminus. He fixes boundaries, the boundaries the Romans crossed when they indulged in excess. Above all, he embodies the boundaries within which their mythology, so rich and so alive, could not be contained.

Pierre BRUNEL

Professeur of Comparative Literature
at the Sorbonne
Member of the Institut Universitaire de France

CONTENTS

AT THE DAWN
OF ROMAN HISTORY

According to the legendary date, Rome was founded in 753 before the common era, yet it did not suddenly spring from nothingness. It took on the appearance first of a small hamlet, then a town, and finally, a modest-sized city among many others, in the heart of Latium, populated by Ligurians, Sabines, Volscians, Samnites, Lucanians, Rutulians and Umbrians, to mention only the most well-known groups. All these peoples could be found in about 9th century BC in the Alban Mountains, southeast of the Tiber River, around a city named Alba Longa. A hundred years later, they began to occupy the future site of Rome and its seven hills, on the banks of the Tiber, where they called themselves by the unifying name of "Latins."

To explain the disappearance of Alba Longa, Livy offered his interpretation of a legend: Alba Longa, founded by Ascanius, the son of Aeneas, was ruled by a dictator named Mettus Suffetius, who was guilty of betraying the Romans. The Romans, then colonised subjects of Alba Longa, revolted against Mettus Suffetius, razed the city and transferred its inhabitants to Rome. This provided an initial account of how Rome came to have a mixed population. Indeed, the city of Rome grew slowly, in several stages.

All the traditions agree that the original city included only Mount Palatine and part of the land located directly below it. It was square-shaped and surrounded by walls. The Sabines had settled on the hills to the north of Mount Palatine, the Quirinal and the Capitoline transformed into a citadel known as Arx. By the 7th century BC, the Etruscans had a huge empire extending around the Mediterranean Basin and all the way up to the northern Atlantic. Their domination spread from the core of their political and administrative power in central Tuscany to Rome, where they settled on Mount Coelius and part of the Esquiline hill.

They occupied these sites for a hundred years before they were incorporated into the nascent Roman state and forced to abandon their position on the hills and build their dwellings in the plain between the Coelius and the Esquiline. The Etruscans exerted a dominant political and religious influence over the small city of Rome. Many of their beliefs and cults were combined with those of the Latins, whose archaeological vestiges – urns and tombs – show they worshipped animals, plants and woods, the first components of a still composite but indigenous religion that would assimilate that of the Greeks later on to form the Roman pantheon.

The royal Rome of the Tarquinians, who reigned until the 4th century BC, quickly developed. Ancus Martius, the fourth king of ancient Rome, who ruled from 640 to 610 BC, took over several Latin cities and transferred the native population, as the first Romans had done with the indigenous population of Alba Longa. They were given Mount Aventinus as their dwelling place. The conquered Latins were incorporated into Rome and became the plebeians.

Ancus Martius also built a fortress on the Janiculus, a hill located on the other side of the Tiber, to protect himself against the Etruscan threat, and connected it to the city by a wooden bridge. Tarquin the Elder who came after him, then Servius Tullius, completed the extension of the city and integrated into it Mount Viminal and Mount Esquiline, surrounding Rome

13

with a line of fortifications that encompassed all the hills, now seven in number. As Rome was slowly built up, it was shaped by varied peoples who, except for the Etruscans, were mainly peasants. They remained faithful to their local and even household gods, whom they continued to worship with the same rites until the end of Rome, a thousand years later. The patricians, who came from the nobility and formed the dominant class, were to become the keepers of this tradition.

Lares

The Romans who founded their city had a special devotion to Lares, which explains why they are the first to be discussed in this essay. They represent the souls of outstanding Romans who marked the history of their city and were consequently the designated protectors of Rome. First and foremost, they watched over the fields and the harvest, inspiring Cicero to write in his *Treatise on Laws* that the sacred woods and countryside were the dwelling place of the Lares. They brought health and happiness to the whole household and were placed in the center of a small altar where they sometimes took the form of "small statuettes, usually made of wax or wood. A portion of the meal was offered to them; they were adorned with garlands and their niches, called Laraia, were left open."

The poet Tibullus sang of them in an *Elegy*: "Watch over and defend me, O Lares of my fathers, you who nourished me when I took my first steps in childhood at your feet. Do not blush at being made of an already aged tree trunk, for thus you lived in the ancient dwelling of my ancestors. The faith was better kept when these gods were made of rough wood and worshipped with simple means in a narrow niche. They could be appeased by nothing more than the offering of a golden grape cluster or having their sacred foreheads adorned with a crown of wheatears. He whose wish was granted by them would bring cakes as an offering, and behind him walked his daughter, holding in her tiny hands a pure beam of honey."

The Lares were governed by a Lar *familiaris*, considered the founder of the family. He remained inseparably attached to the family and followed them whenever they moved to a new dwelling. Lares were such an integral part of the home that they became its very essence, so much so that when Romans were without a place to live, they said that had no Lar. Lares were so important that Plautus, the famous author of

burlesque comedies, made one a character in his play Aulularia, who speaks out as early as the prologue: "I am the Lar god of the house which you just saw me leaving. I have been its guardian for many years, from one generation to the next, until today, I have been watching over it."

Lares were not only of prime importance in every Roman household; they also protected the city of Rome and, in so doing, played an official role. They were called Lares *compitales*, for they were placed at the *compita*, i.e. the crossroads or the place where two or more streets came together. Their statuettes were placed in an open shrine or on an altar. They were celebrated at the feast of the Compitalia where the humble folk gathered together around the cult of the guardians of the crossroads and, consequently, of communication and trade.

In *Roman Religion from Augustus to the Antonines*, Gaston Boissier evokes the atmosphere of these festivities in honor of the public Lares, which usually took place in early January: "The residents of the quarter formed an association with a common treasury and a president, and for three days the entire neighborhood gaily attended shows by wandering players, contests between athletes and all sorts of entertainment. The lower classes took great pleasure in the feast, which provided amusement for workers, slaves and all those whose lives were hard and devoid of distractions."

The Roman authorities were wary of the celebrations, which they were not always able to control, and Caesar had them outlawed. Emperor Augustus reinstated them, but only by connecting the Lares to his own person and giving them the name Lares *Augusti*: the Lares of Augustus.

Soldiers and sailors, the conquering forces of the Roman State, also had their own Lares who ensured their protection. These Lares were the focus of public prayers and sacrifices, especially in time of war. Similarly, the Lares *praestites*, a sort of avant-garde who went ahead and protected the entire city, were seen as watchful sentinels against the enemy. Ovid wrote about them in the *Fasti*: "During the calends of May, an altar was raised in honor of the Lares *praestites* and the statues of these gods were consecrated [...]. The nickname given to these gods when the cult was first established comes from the fact that their watchful gaze protects everything we possess. They also watch over us,

and oversee the security of our walls; they are present everywhere, and everywhere ready to come to our help. At their feet stands a dog carved out of the same stone. Why is this dog with the Lar? Together, they guard the house, both are faithful to their master; the crossroads are pleasing to the god, as they are pleasing to the dogs. The Lar and Diana's pack of hounds harass and hunt thieves. Watchful are the dogs and watchful the Lares. I looked for the statues of these twin gods, worn out after so many years; today the city has a thousand Lares and the genius of the leader who gave them to us (the Emperor Augustus)."

Macrobius asserts in the *Saturnalia* that the mother of the Lares is Mania, who is considered the goddess of madness. "For some time," he even claims, "children were immolated in honor of the goddess Mania, mother of the Lares, in order to save the family.

After the Tarquins were expelled (i.e. at the end of royalty in Rome in the 5th century BC), the consul Junius Brutus ordered these sacrifices to be celebrated in another way. Instead of committing the crime of sacrilegious immolation, he ordered the offering of heads of garlic and poppy (to the goddess, mother of the Lares). [...] The custom was established that whenever a family was threatened with danger, they could ward it off it by hanging an effigy of Mania on the front door of the house."

Penates

Along with the Lares in Roman households, there were also a pair of gods known as Penates. Their etymology indicates both their importance and their function: the name comes from penus which means "larder" and penetralia or "pantry." A perpetual flame was kept burning in their honor and the table was always dedicated to them so that the food and drink would be abundant. They were entitled to a special place around the table where salt, flowers and fruit were laid as offerings, and the head of the family offered a bit of each dish to the Penates, before distributing it to his wife, children and the other members of the household.

The cult of the Penates, like that of the Lares, was also taken over by the Roman State and each city had its public Penates. According to legend, they were first brought from Troy by Aeneas to Lanuvium and Alba in Italy, and later to Rome. They were sometimes identified with Romulus and Remus, the founders of Rome, or with the Diocuri, Castor and Pollux, the twin sons of Jupiter

and Leda. Legend has it that the latter played an important role in the battle between the Romans and the Latins on the shores of Lake Regilla in Latium in 498 BC.

In Rome, national Penates were honored in a temple called the Regia, in the center of the Forum, which housed the city's religious administration, along with a number of temples, one dedicated to Mars, the god of war, and the other to Ops, the goddess of abundance. Augustus, who was always eager to re-establish the ancient Roman religion and lost traditions, had a sanctuary dedicated to the Penates of the city of Rome erected in his palace on Mount Palatine.

Vesta

In addition to daily worship of the Lares and the Penates, the cult of Vesta, the goddess of the hearth and the feminine personification of fire, was practised in the center of the home.

Every day, the entire household gathered together to worship by sharing a meal as a sign of unity and affection among all the members of the same family, and as a tribute to Vesta, to whom meat or bread was sacrificed. In 2 BC, Cato the Elder recommended in his *Treatise on Agriculture* that the head of the family should watch over the hearth, keep it clean, walk around it every night before going to bed, and decorate it three times a month with a crown of flowers, on the calends, ides and nones, each time in honor of Vesta. Consequently, every home was a temple of Vesta all by itself.

While Vesta was honored privately in every Roman dwelling, she was also publicly worshipped by the Roman State for political purposes. The temple of Vesta stood in the Forum between Mount Capitoline and Mount Palatine, not far from the temple of the Penates. Ovid wrote in his *Fasti* that the temple "has not a single angle jutting out, and is sheltered from water and rain by a dome." The goddess was not represented in the temple by a statue, but by a perpetual flame, a living symbol, that burned on the altar. The fire was kept alive by Vestals, virgin priestesses like the goddess herself.

"You ask why the goddess wants virgins as ministers of her altars," writes Ovid in the *Fasti*. Here, I will tell you the truth. It is said that Saturn first made Ops the mother of Juno and Ceres; Vesta was the third-born; the first two became wives and had children in turn; only the youngest refused to yield to the embrace of a husband. It is hardly surprising that, as a virgin herself, she should want virgins as priestesses, entrusting to their chaste hands the care of her sanctuary. Indeed, what is Vesta if not an ardent fire? Yet fire has never engendered anything. It is thus right that she should be a virgin and surround herself with virgin companions, she who neither gives nor receives a single germ of life."

If one of the Vestal virgins failed to keep her vows of chastity, she was walled up alive until she died. Every year on the first of March, the sacred fire of Vesta and the laurel tree that shaded her hearth were replaced, and on the fifteenth of June, her temple was cleaned and purified. Any waste was transported to a sort of cellar closed off by a door that no one could enter.

The first half of the day on which the ceremony took place was considered unlucky and even the priestess of Juno, a goddess who also played a role in protecting the heart of the Roman State, was not allowed to comb her hair or trim her fingernails.

During the second half of the day, on the other hand, drawing up marriage contracts or undertaking important affairs was thought to be advisable. Just a few days before this solemn occasion, women were allowed to enter the temple, alone and barefooted: "For a long time, in my ignorance," adds Ovid, "I believed that there were statues of Vesta. Not long ago, I learned that there are none in her temple, where only a fire is kept and never allowed to go out, with no images of either the fire or of Vesta."

Later on, the poet examines the origins of the word Vesta, asserting: "As for the hearth, it was given the name because of the flames, and because it warmed everything. In olden times, it was placed in the rear part of the house; hence, in my opinion, it is the source of the word "vestibule" and of the words contained in the prayers to Vesta: "O Vesta, thou who occupiest the leading place…"

Manes

Alongside the divinities that protected life and the living, there were others who watched over death and the dead. Thus, the Manes were genuine gods who were paid tribute in all the funerary inscriptions of ancient, pagan Rome: "Diis Manibus": "To the Manes gods". They stood for the immortality of souls, the spirit of the dead and their familiarity with those left behind on earth.

The cult rendered to them testifies to their importance. On the ninth day of the funeral for the deceased, a thanksgiving ceremony took place during which special dishes were served. Flowers that they

particularly appreciated, especially anemones, roses, myrtle, violets and lilies, were placed or planted on top of tombs. The Manes breathed in the fragrance from the flowers. They were also fond of familiar foods such as honey, wine, milk, eggs, lentils and fava beans that the relatives of the deceased placed at the burial ground.

Over the ages, the Manes became less demanding, as Ovid explains in the *Fasti*: "The Manes are content with very little. They consider piety alone the richest of gifts; there is no greed or cupidity among the divinities of the Styx (that is, the Underworld). It is enough to hide the funerary tile beneath the wreaths, and add some wheat, a few grains of salt and bread softened by wine; a few scattered violets, all together in a vase left in the middle of the path. You may, if you so desire, add further solemnity to your tributes; but the ones just mentioned will suffice for the Manes. Again pronounce the prayers and established words before the embers of their altars."

Later on, Ovid adds further specific details on the worship of the Manes, a proof of their primordial importance in Roman religion: "Towards the middle of the night, when silence encourages sleep, and one no longer hears the barking of dogs nor various bird songs, the man who has remained faithful to the ancient rites and fears the gods shall get up; no shoes shall cover his feet. With his fingers joined to the thumb, he sends the signal to chase away the light shadows, for fear they might rise up in front of him if he should walk noiselessly. Three times shall he wash his hands in the water of a fountain; he turns and puts black fava beans in his mouth; then he drops them behind him saying: 'I throw away these fava beans, and thereby redeem myself and my family.' Nine times shall he pronounce these words without looking behind him; according to his beliefs, the shadow picks them up and follows his footsteps without being glimpsed."

"Again, he plunges his hands into the water and rings the bronze from Temsa (a city in Brutium with copper mines): he entreats the shadow to leave his roof; and after repeating nine times: 'Come out, Paternal Manes!' he looks behind him, and thinks that he has accomplished all the rites of the ceremony."

The cult of the Manes was so important that any interruption was dreadful for the city, as Ovid recounts, again in the *Fasti*: "Once, during a time of long and bloody wars, it happened that the days dedicated to the Manes of the ancestors were not celebrated. The

vengeance was swift, and after this sacrilegious neglect, so many pyres were lighted in the outskirts that the heat could be felt even in the city. It is said that an amazing wonder occurred: the Manes of the ancestors came out of their tombs and set about moaning in lamentation in the silence of the night; it is said that this lugubrious band of elusive ghosts frightened the streets of Rome and the countryside of Latium with their wailing. The honors demanded by the shadows and tombs were finally paid; the spirits disappeared and death ceased its ravages."

The Genius

In addition to the household cults, which were essential to Roman religion, there was also the cult of the Genius.

Every man was helped at birth by a Genius. Women, on the other hand, were deprived of a Genius and Juno served as a sort of guardian angel for them. The guardian spirit, which seems to have been handed down to the Romans by the Etruscans, though its etymological origins connect it to the term generator or father, was worshipped in particular on birthdays, with libations of wine, incense and garlands of flowers. The nuptial bed was also dedicated to the Genius.

On other happy occasions, sacrifices were offered to the Genius in the form of offerings of wine, flowers, cakes and incense. Whenever people experienced joy or happiness in their lives, they invoked their Genius to give thanks. Genii were usually represented in artworks as winged creatures. In the course of Roman antiquity, the Genius took on the appearance of a man dressed in a toga, holding a patera and a cornucopia in his hands. Places, too, had their Genii, which often took the form of a snake eating fruit placed before it.

Apart from the private Genii of families, ancestors and individual households, there was a Genius of the city of Rome, called the public Genius of the Roman people, who was asked to protect Rome in times of peril and on the eve of combat, by offering him many sacrifices at the Capitol. This Genius was represented on coins as an old, bearded man with the initials G.P.R. (Genius of the Roman People) engraved above. A temple was also dedicated to this Genius.

Finally, under the Roman Empire, there was the Genius of the emperor, a sacred Spirit that dwelled within the sovereign and was identified with the Lares of Augustus. He, too, received libations at numerous shrines in all the quarters of Rome.

A Genius

This Genius, an innocent little child, weeps over death, which is symbolised by the flame of life that goes out when he overturns his torch.
Jean-Baptiste Defermex,
1729-1783

NATIONAL DIVINITIES

Agricultural gods

Prior to the Roman conquest of Greece and the introduction of the twelve Olympian gods into the Roman pantheon, there were many specific, indigenous gods that had no equivalent anywhere else in the Mediterranean Basin.

At every moment, not to say every instant, in their daily lives, the Romans were duty-bound to put themselves under the protection of a divinity, thereby increasing their number. These gods were, in fact, considered to be sacred, higher powers and were not always represented. They were given the generic name of *numen*.

The Romans referred to hundreds of numen and had to find ways of reconciling the favors they bestowed. Lists of numen, drawn up by the priests, were circulated so that everyone would know who was who.

There were many national gods, and the Romans never confused them with those gradually imported from their conquests. Indeed, the national gods differed from the "foreign" gods by their natural, rough, spontaneous character, totally lacking in literary, theogonic, cosmological or mythological adornment, though they were gradually incorporated into the system of Roman mythology and assigned an appearance and legends. Originally, they were merely an figment of the imagination of the Romans, a people of peasants and foot soldiers, arising from their contact with nature.

The most important ones were those that marked the rhythm of agricultural activities and watched over the prosperity of trade.

All a farmer needed to know was that he should call upon Sterculinus, who fertilised the earth, Vervactor who cleared the land for cultivation, Redarator who did the spadework, Sator who sowed and Occator who harrowed. This gives an idea of how difficult, not to say impossible, it would be to mention all these divinities by name and describe their specific functions.

We shall therefore limit ourselves to the most important among them, presented in Latin alphabetical order to make them more readily accessible.

Acca Larentia

Acca Larentia was the wife of the shepherd Faustulus and the nurse of Romulus and Remus. She brought twelve sons into the world, the Arvales brothers, whom she led in a procession around the fields every year with sacrifices to make the earth fertile. When one of them died, Romulus took his place and established the priestly college of the Arvales Brothers.

There is another version of the story of Acca Larentia recounted by Macrobius in the *Saturnalia*: "It is said," he wrote, "that under the reign of Ancus Martius (the fourth king of Rome, who reigned in the middle of the 7th century BC), the guardian of the temple of Hercules, finding himself idle during the festivities of Jupiter called *Larentiales*, challenged the god to a game of dice, holding both hands himself, on condition that the loser should treat the winner to supper and a courtesan."

"When Hercules won, the guardian closed the temple with supper inside, as well as Acca Larentia, a famous courtesan of the period. The next day, she spread the rumour that, after lying with the god, she was told her reward would come by accepting the first occasion on her way home." "It so happened that, shortly after she left the temple, Carucius, struck by her beauty, called out to her. She yielded to his desires and he married her. Upon the death of her husband, Acca Larentia came into possession of his property and she made the Roman people her heir after her death."

"For this reason, Ancus had her buried in the Velabrus, a famous place in the city, where a solemn sacrifice was offered by a priest to the Manes gods of Acca Larentia."

Cato the Elder added, according to Macrobius, that Acca "became rich through her trade as a courtesan,

and after her death, left the fields called Turax, Semurium, Luttrium and Solinium to the Roman people, and because of this, she was honored with a magnificent tomb and an annual funeral ceremony," the *Larentalia*, on the 23rd of December.

It is also said that, as one of the most beautiful women in the world, she was the stakes of a game of dice between the guardian of the temple of Hercules and Hercules himself. Hercules won the game and seduced her. He was the one who is said to have advised her to marry a rich Etruscan and thereby, become rich.

Abundantia

Abundantia or Abundance, as her name suggests, watched over prosperity and wealth. She was usually represented with a cornucopia, the horn coming from the goat of Amaltheia that fed Jupiter. She generously distributed grain and coins.

Consus

Consus, a very ancient Roman divinity, was no doubt agrarian, for her feast was celebrated on the 21st of August, after the harvest, and then on the 15th of December, after sowing. The ceremonies were held in a temple erected in her honor in the Great Circus of Rome.

Varro, in his *Treatise on the Latin Language*, explains that the *Consualia*, the feast in honor of Consus, were celebrated by priests who gave a dramatic representation of the rape of the Sabine women in a circus around the altar.

According to Tacitus, in his *Annals*, one of the markers placed in front of the altar of Consus recalled a boundary marker of the city of Rome, as it was drawn by Romulus' plow.

Faunus

Faunus, grandson of the god Saturn and father of Latinus, was originally king of Laurentius. After his death, like many legendary kings in Rome, he was proclaimed divine and worshipped as a protector of agriculture and shepherds against attacks by wolves.

He was sometimes honored under the name of Lupercus and celebrated at the festival of the *Lupercales*, represented as a small, sturdy man with a beard and a crown of leaves on his head, dressed in goatskin, with a club or cornucopia as his emblem, and sometimes with horns and goats hooves like the Greek god Pan.

What Faunus was to men, Fauna, his wife, was to women. She watched over their fertility and the harmonious workings of human reproduction.

In his *Treatise on the Latin Language*, Varro claimed that both lived in the woods and foretold the future in verses called "saturnians", hence the word "Faunus" which comes from *fari* meaning "to tell."

There are a number of pleasant, licentious stories about Faunus, some of which are told by Ovid in the *Fasti*: "One day," he writes, "Hercules was accompanying the queen (Omphale), his mistress. Faunus spied them from a hilltop, and instantly enflamed by a thousand fires, he said, 'Farewell, nymphs of the mountains, farewell; behold the one I wish henceforth to love.'

When night fell, he approached the cave where Hercules lay beside Omphale. But the hero had donned the garments of the queen, and the queen had put on those of the hero. Faunus unsuspectingly "entered, a bold adulterer, directing his steps here and there. [...] He arrived at the desired bed [...] smelled the soft, thin fabric, and taken in by false appearances [...] began gently to pull back the tunic: the legs that it covered were bristling with rough hairs. Hercules pushed him back with his elbow and he fell noisily to the ground. The queen called for her ladies-in-waiting, asking them to bring torches; immediately torches were brought, lighting up the scene. The god Faunus was moaning, bruised from his heavy fall, and could barely raise his crushed limbs [...]"

Everyone burst out laughing and, says Ovid: "Since that time, the god can no longer bear the perfidious garments that caused his error. He wants those who come before his altars to be naked."

Felicitas

Felicitas or Felicity was the personification of happiness, of good events and the fertility of the land. She was represented on Roman coins and medals holding a patera or a caduceus.

Feronia

Feronia, a name of Sabine origin, was one of many very ancient Italian rustic divinities. Celebrated in Preneste, Capene and Terracine near Mount Soracte, she watched over forests and also protected emancipated slaves. She was represented as a woman wearing a crown with radiating light.

Faunus

To the right, Dionysus or Bacchus, with his crown of vine branches, and Pan or Faunus with his goat hooves and horns, both of them related to many feasts and cults devoted to rustic divinities.
Roman bronze.
2nd century CE

In the *Aeneid*, Virgil speaks of her when King Evander, the Latin king on Mount Palatine, was forced to kill King Herilus "to whom the nymph Feronia, his mother, had given at his birth – O horrible wonder! – three souls and three suits of armor. He had to be struck thrice with a mortal blow," which Evander succeeded in doing, though not without difficulty.

Flora

As a very ancient Italic goddess, Flora reigned over springtime and its most colorful expression, with flowers that she helped to blossom and fruit she helped to multiply.

She was the wife of Favonus, the wind of the west and of the rain that enables trees and plants to find the water they need to grow. The *Floralia*, festivals dedicated to Flora, took place from the 28th of April to the 1st of May in the heart of springtime, and they were known for their debauchery and licentiousness. Ovid writes of them in the *Fasti*:

"I salute you, goddess of the flowers, you whose feast brings back frolicking games. The solemnities of your cult begin in April and continue into May. These two months encompass you, the first one in its final days, the second in its first."

Ovid went on: "The goddess speaks to me and from her mouth the soft fragrance of spring roses exhales, as she says these words: 'She whom you call Flora was once Chloris; one letter of my name was changed when it went from the Greeks to the Latins."

"I was Chloris, nymph of the wealthy regions, where you know that men lived out their lives in the bosom of felicity. To tell you how beautiful I was would tarnish my modesty: if my mother had a god for her son-in-law, it was due to this beauty. It was in springtime, I was wandering about by chance. Zephyr, one of the wind gods, saw me. I moved away but he followed me. I tried in vain to flee, I could not struggle against him... Yet Zephyr made up for his fault by making me his wife and no further complaint arose from our marriage bed."

"I delight in the springtime: the year keeps all of its wealth for me, the tree its foliage and the earth its greenery. The fields I received as my dowry contain a fertile garden, caressed by the breath of the wind and watered by the clear water of a fountain. My husband filled it with the most magnificent flowers and said to me: 'Goddess, you shall reign over these flowers. Often have I wished to classify and count their colors, but I never succeeded: their multitude is so great that no number would be enough. As soon as the leaves have shaken off the cold drops of dew and the varied stems have warmed beneath the rays of the sun, I see the Hours come running in their variegated gowns; they gather my gifts in light baskets; the Graces carry them off immediately to plait garlands and wreaths that blend with the hair of the gods."

"I was the first to scatter unknown seeds over the vast surface of the universe […] Perhaps you think that my empire extends only to flowers that are woven into delicate garlands; the countryside, too, acknowledges my divinity. If the wheat has blossomed well, the barns will be full; if the vines have blossomed well, you shall have wine; if the olives have blossomed well, the year will produce a thousand treasures; and finally the richness of autumn merely keeps the promises of the season that belongs to me. […] Honey is one of my gifts; it is I who call the honey-giving bee to the violet and the laburnum and to the thick branches of thyme. Finally, it is I who reign over the beautiful years of youth when life is overflowing, and the body has all its strength."

In modest, metaphorical, even hidden terms, Ovid evokes the licentious games and feasts that were, in fact, orgies, which were dedicated to Flora:

"I wished to ask why the license was greater and the jokes bolder in these games. I remembered that Flora was not a strict divinity, and that her gifts served to adorn our pleasures. Foreheads were crowned with a fabric of flowers; splendid tables disappeared beneath a rain of roses. Guests, their hair circled with garlands holding strands of lime-blossom, danced, excited by the wine vapors, and in their chaotic movements, they followed no other master than drunkenness. Lovers, drunk as well, sang before the inexorable threshold of their beautiful mistresses. Light crowns blended with perfumed hair. […] But why should the crowd of courtesans celebrate this solemn occasion? It is easy to see the reason. Flora is not a gloomy divinity. Along with serious teachings, she also wants plebeian joy to burst forth freely at her festivals. She invites us to enjoy the beautiful age, while it is in bloom."

Ovid continues his dialogue with Flora: "Why," he asks the goddess, "is it customary to wear many-colored costumes at these festivals, as white garments are worn at the feast of *Cereales*?"

"Could it be because the ear of wheat whitens when it begins to ripen, whereas the varied hues of flowers are countless?"

"The goddess assented with a nod of the head and blossoms fell from her bowed forehead, as upon the tables of our feasts we let fall a rain of flowers."

"There remained only to learn why torches were lighted. The goddess dispelled my doubts in this way: 'The use of torches was established on the days of my festival, either because the country seemed to be lit up by the bright colors of the flowers, or because a burst of brightness is the attribute of flowers as of flame and through their splendid appearance, they also attract our gaze. Or finally because night time favors the free pursuit of our pleasures and the facts indeed lend truth to this third explanation.' [...] She spoke no more and vanished into the air, leaving behind a fragrance that betrayed the passage of an immortal."

Liber

Liber, also known by the name of Liber Pater, is a very ancient Italic divinity who reigned over the cultivation of vines and the fertility of the fields.

A god of the earth, often confused with Ceres or Proserpina or identified with the Greek god Dionysus, he was celebrated, along with his female counterpart, Liberia, at the feast of the *Liberalia* on March 17. In the *Fasti*, Ovid says in this connection that a poor old woman invited the people to buy honey cakes and she broke a piece off each one as an offering on the altar of the god Liber.

Similarly, Ovid adds, children receive the toga on the day of the feast of this "god of dazzling beauty." No doubt, he concludes, this is because the god is called Liber and taking the toga also means that one intends to live with greater freedom. The symbol of Liber is the phallus, which is invoked to ensure the fertility not only of the fields but also of the herds.

Lupercus

Lupercus also belongs to the set of ancient Italian rustic gods. Like Faunus, with whom he is sometimes identified, as we saw earlier, he protects the herds from the attacks of wolves and consequently, ensures the prosperity of the peasantry. He was celebrated on the *Lupercales*, a major feast in Rome, held on the 15th of February. These feasts, recounted by Ovid in the *Fasti*, originated in the following legend: "It was at the festival of goat-footed Faunus, after a goat had been sacrificed according to custom, and everyone had come forward for his frugal share of the feast. While the priests set out for the meal the entrails of the victim on willow spits, Romulus and his brother, along with the young shepherds, ran naked beneath the shining sun that had reached the midpoint of its daily race. That was when Remus had to fight against the thieves who had carried off the meat and he succeeded in driving them away."

"The trace of this event still subsists; the race without clothes has established the memory of Remus' success." It is also true that during the festival of the *Lupercales*, the young people ran through Rome, wearing goatskins that left nothing about their bodies to the imagination.

The name "Luperques", again according to Ovid's *Fasti*, is also an allusion to the she-wolf who had taken in the twins Romulus and Remus and fed them with her milk on the banks of the Tiber and "gave her name to this place which gave its name to the Luperques themselves." This festival also consisted in the flagellation of sterile women by priests in order to make them fertile, like the she-wolf, with her teats full of milk originally intended for her dead cubs, which gave strength to the abandoned twins. This legend is told in greater detail under Romulus.

Ops

Ops, a Sabine divinity, was the wife of Saturn. She saw to it that grain grew in the fields and therefore, that the harvests were abundant. Farmers celebrated her feast day on the 25th of August, right after the harvest, and on the 19th of December, after sowing.

She appears on coins in the effigy of a woman seated on a throne, with a sceptre or a globe and wheat ears in her hands. In his *Treatise on the Latin Language*, Varro says that in the beginning "the earth was called *ops*, because all work was done on the earth and she was needed (*opus* means "work") in order to live.

From there the name of mother given to Ops and to the Earth. "Indeed, the earth gives birth to the animals, feeds them and receives them, after death, in her bosom", wrote Ennius, a Roman poet of the 2nd century BC, of whose works we have only a few remaining fragments.

Pales

Pales was one of the divinities of the shepherds and herds. It should be noted that the etymology of her name is the same as that of Palatine, to show clearly that

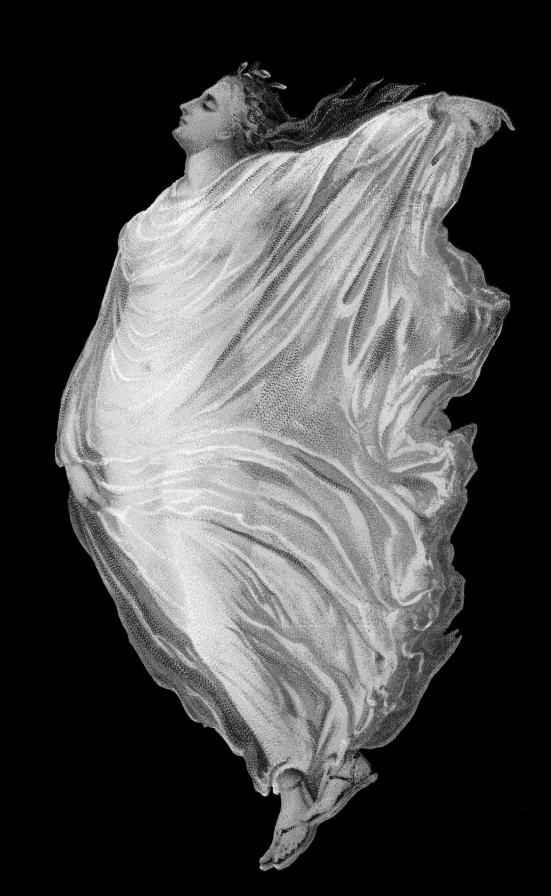

the city was set up and inhabited in the beginning by peasants and that Romulus used a plow to mark out its limits.

In Ovid's *Fasti*, he evokes the *Palilies*, the festivals devoted to the goddess on the 21st of April, the legendary date of the founding of Rome, to insist on her importance. It is worth quoting at length, if only to give an accurate, detailed example of these agricultural and rural Italic and Italiot cults, to which the Romans were especially attached, and attenuate the legend of a Roman pantheon copied exclusively from that of the Greeks.

"Night has disappeared, dawn is breaking. The Palilies call upon the poet. The poet will respond if the beneficent Pales should come to my aid. O Pales, inspire he who would sing of pastoral festivals, if he has always shown pious zeal in venerating you. I can say that I have often carried firmly in my hands the ashes of sacrificial calves and fava stems, chaste expiatory offerings. I leaped over three rows of rosebushes close together and spread the lustral waters with a laurel branch. The goddess Pales allows herself to be touched and is willing to help me. [...].. People, go and seek the expiatory offerings on the virginal altar." [...]

"These offerings will be the blood of a horse, the ashes of a calf, and thirdly, the bare stem of hardened fava beans. Shepherds, spread the lustral waters over your sated ewes at the first light of dawn. Let the water begin by irrigating the earth and a tree branch sweep over it. Adorn the sheepfold with branches and foliage; let the doors be shaded and decorated with a long garland. Let pure sulphur throw an azure flame. Let the smoke reaching the ewes make them bleat. Burn the male olive tree, the resinous torch and the Sabine grasses. Let the laurel tree sparkle as it burns in the midst of the hearth."

"Let the basket woven with millet accompany the millet cakes: this is the favorite food of the rustic Pales. Add to it the consecrated food and warm, freshly drawn milk. Divide up the food, offer up the warm milk and invoke Pales who enjoys the forests. 'Protect', you must ask her, 'both the herds and the masters of the herd. Let my stable be the scene of no disaster. If my herd should enter a sacred pasture, if I am seated beneath a sacred tree, if my sheep have inadvertently grazed upon the grass of graves, if I enter a forbidden wood, if my presence has sent the nymphs or the goat-footed god (Faunus) fleeing, if my sickle has stripped a sacred wood of a few branches in the deep darkness to give fresh foliage to a stricken sheep, forgive me.' If, while hailstones fell, I found shelter for my sheep in some country sanctuary, if I have troubled the lakes, do not punish me, nymphs, forgive me. Forget that my herds brought the silt up from the riverbed into your limpid waters. [...]"

"Keep illnesses at bay, preserve the health of the men and the herds and the cautious pack of our watchful dogs. Let me count as many heads in the evening as I counted in the morning, let me not sigh as I carry back fleece torn from the teeth of wolves. Protect us from the horrors of famine. Let there be an abundance of grass and foliage. Let water be not lacking either to wash the body or quench our thirst. Let my hand press swollen teats and my cheese bring me plenty of money. Let the whey drain through wide racks."

"Let the ram be ardent and the female conceive and be fertile. Let my stables be peopled with young lambs, let me gather soft wool that cannot wound the hand of a young girl and can be spun by the most delicate fingers. Let our wishes be granted and every year, we shall offer large cakes to Pales, goddess of the shepherds. Only thus can the goddess be made propitious."

Picus

Picus or Woodpecker was originally a prophetic Latin divinity, the son of Saturn, husband of Canens and father of Faunus. The legend of Picus is based on the idea that the woodpecker is a prophetic bird, dedicated to Mars, the god of war.

In the land of Aeques, a woodpecker used to pronounce oracles, perched on the top of a column. That is why Picus was first represented as a large tree trunk with a woodpecker on top. Like many Italiot divinities, he protected agriculture and marriage, both of them a proof of fertility.

In The *Metamorphoses*, Ovid tells the legend of Picus, when the nymph, a companion of the famous magician, Circe, showed him the white marble statue of Picus, the head of which, adorned with many crowns, had a woodpecker on top. "Picus, son of Saturn," she told him, "reigned in Ausonia. He had a passion for training valiant messengers for war. This statue is his: you can see in this marble image how beautiful he was and that his soul was as beautiful as his face. [...]."

"One nymph only received his love: Canante, the daughter of twin-faced Janus and Venilia, who brought

him to life on Mount Palatine. The nymph's singing was so marvellous that she even cast a spell on the animals of the woods and forests."

"One day, while she was pleased to make her melodious voice heard, Picus came out of his palace to go boar hunting in the countryside of Laurentius. He spurred his fiery horse onward; two javelins shone in his left hand and one golden clasp held up the folds of his purple tunic.

That same day, the daughter of the Sun (the magician Circe herself) had left her island to come to the same forests, on the fertile hills of Laurentius, to pick new plants. Hidden in the bushes, she spied Picus. She stood still with surprise, and dropped the flowers she had gathered. Fire coursed through her veins."

She had barely recovered from her initial emotion when she wanted to speak to him and confess all her desires.

But the king's young horse carried him swiftly away amid a whirlwind of hunters. 'You will not escape me,' she cried. 'No, not even if you were carried off by the wind. No, if I know myself, if all the virtues of the plants have not vanished, if all my entreaties have not deceived my expectations.' Thus she spoke and the shadow of a boar, a disembodied image, passed beneath the eyes of Picus, and seemed to disappear into the thick woods, through a thicket so vigorous that the horses could not penetrate it."

"At that moment, the hunter, taken in, jumped down from his steaming steed, ran after the imaginary prey and lost his way in the depths of the forest. Circe murmured diabolical prayers. [...] At the sound of these terrible words, a dark night covered the sky. The earth exhaled black vapors. The king's companions became lost in the shadows and left him by himself. The goddess seized the opportunity and moment: 'Oh, by the shining eyes that captivated mine,' she said to Picus, 'by that adorable beauty which makes me a goddess, I beg you on my knees."

'Take pity on my fire, receive as your wife the daughter of the Sun, whose gaze sets the universe ablaze. Let yourself be touched by my prayers; do not scorn the love of Circe!' But Picus proudly repulsed the goddess and her wishes: 'Whoever you may be,' he said, 'I cannot belong to you: another possesses me and may she possess me forever! No, never, as long as the gods keep for me the daughter of Janus, no other love will come to violate the vow that unites us!

Circe begged and beseeched him again, but in vain. Then she cried out in fury: "Your insolence will not go unpunished! You shall never see Canens again: you shall learn what a woman, an offended lover, can do, especially when that woman is Circe who loves you and whom you have gravely offended."

"Then, she turned twice towards the East, twice towards the West: she touched Picus thrice with her wand and three times she pronounced magic words over him. He fled, astonishing himself with the speed of his running, but he saw that he had wings. He had become a new bird in the forests of Latium. Indignant, he struck the trees with a beak as hard as steel. Enraged, he made deep wounds in their branches. His plumage had kept the purple of his tunic; and the bright yellow of his golden clasp shone around his neck. Nothing remained of Picus but his name."

Picmunus and Pilmunus

Picmunus and Pilmunus were the rustic gods of marriage in Roman religion, and hence the guardians of the well being of children at birth and more generally of agriculture, as a sign of the fecundity of nature.

In the *Aeneid*, Virgil has him marry Danae, the heroine of Greek mythology whom Jupiter visited in the form of golden rain and who gave birth to Perseus nine months later.

The Latin poet was therefore following an Italian version of the legend: Danae had boarded ship in Italy after her father had imprisoned her along with her child in a trunk and thrown it into the sea, and had built the city of Ardea, capital of Rutulians in Latium.

From her marriage to Pilumnus, she had a son, Daunus.

Danus married the nymph Venilia, the sister of Amata, the king of Latium, engendering the nymph Juturna and Turnus, king of the Rutulians, upon the arrival of Aeneas in Italy, thereby complying with the ancient Roman epic tradition that maintained all great men of state were of divine lineage.

Pomona

Pomona watched over the fertility of fruit trees. In *The Metamorphoses*, Ovid depicts her this way: " Among the Hamadryads of Latium, none was more skilful in cultivating gardens; none knew more about fruit trees; hence her name of Pomona [*pomum* means "apple" or "fruit" in Latin].

"She loves neither the forests nor the rivers, but rather the fields and the trees that bend low beneath their happy abundance."

"Her hand is not armed with a javelin, but with a light pruning knife to trim the branches of a disorderly shoot or to repress useless luxuriance or to split the bark on which she grafts a foreign bud that the trunk will nourish with its sap. Never have her trees suffered from thirst; she brings to their feet the streams that water the thirsty fibers of their roots. These are her tastes, her pleasures; she does not think about love."

"To avoid the pursuit of country gods, she closes her orchards with care; she anticipates and flees their approach. They have left nothing untried in their efforts to vanquish her, the leaping satyrs and pine-crowned fauns as well as Sylvanus, ever young in his advanced age." However, in Ovid's *Metamorphoses*, after many vicissitudes, she is given Vertumnus, the god of vegetable gardens, as her husband.

Priapus

Priapus was a sexual god, hence the name priapism, an affliction that prevents men from hiding their desire for women. His task was to ensure the fertility of herds of sheep and goats, bees and more generally, everything produced by gardens.

He watched over the quality of the semen of billy goats and rams, queen bees and pollination. With such powers, it is easy to understand why Roman mythology made ruddy Priapus, celebrated for the size of his manly attributes, the rough and robust seducer of women and goddesses, often at his own expense.

Ovid tells an anecdote on this subject in the *Fasti*. "Cybele, who wears a high crown upon her forehead, invited the immortal gods to her feasts. She also asked satyrs and nymphs, divinities of the countryside. Silenus came as well, though no one had invited him. It is not for me to recount this feast of the gods, and furthermore, it would take too long. Abundant libations lent a charm to the night hours."

"Some wandered at random in the dark valleys of Ida, others stretched out to rest on the soft grass, and still others slept. Some joined arms and kept the rhythm by light-footed tapping on the green-adorned earth. Vesta lay down and safely yielded to the sweetness of sleep, her head posed carelessly against a grassy bank."

"The ruddy guardian, coveted by nymphs and goddesses, wandered to and fro. He spied Vesta. Did he take her for a nymph or did he recognise her as Vesta? We do not know. Priapus declared he did not recognise her. A lustful desire awakened in him and he furtively came closer.

His foot barely touched the ground and his heart was hammering violently. As chance would have it, the donkey brought by Silenus had been left at the edge of the babbling brook. Priapus was about to accomplish his purpose when the donkey began to bray in an untimely fashion. At this resounding voice, the goddess awoke with a start. A large crowd came running to her side. Priapus escaped from vengeful hands only by fleeing."

Robigo

Robigo or Robigus. According to some Latin authors, this divinity had her own cult in Rome because she was thought to protect the young ears of wheat against diseases such as wheat rust and drought.

The festival of the *Robigalia*, dedicated to the goddess, took place on April 25, at a time when the wheatears were forming and in bloom. A ewe and a dog were sacrificed, and as frequently occurred at agrarian festivals, this one ended with a few orgies to signify the strength of the sap and of fertility.

It is said that King Numa established the cult of Robigo shortly after the founding of Rome. In the *Fasti*, Ovid proposes a prayer for the occasion designed to rid the fields of wheat rust and celebrate the Pax Romana promoted by Emperor Augustus.

Henceforth, rust would attack only weapons: "Fatal goddess of rust, spare the nascent ears of wheat; allow their polished stems to wave above the furrows; let the harvest that prospered under the favorable influence of auspicious constellations grow until they are cut down by the reaper's scythe. Your power is great, and at the sight of wheat that has suffered from your attacks, the farmer sighs, sadly thinking that they are irreparably lost. The wind and rain are less harmful to the treasures of Ceres; frost with its white wintry weather that burns them and alters their gold is less to be feared than the sun that warms the damp stems. It is then, O fearsome goddess, that your wrath bursts forth."

"Take pity, I beg of you! Do not touch our harvests with your rough hands; spare our tillage; let your power to harm suffice. Instead of attacking the tender crops, gnaw hard iron, and first consume this destructive metal. Is it not preferable to destroy man-slaying swords and javelins? We no longer wish to use them and the universe longs for rest. From now on, let the wealth of the countryside, the weeding instruments and hoes and curved plowshares alone shimmer in the sun! Let all weapons be lost to rust and may the sword be riveted to its sheath by long years of peace, and resist the efforts of anyone who tries to pull it out."

Silvanus

Silvanus was a very ancient divinity of the fields, woods, farms and large rural properties. He also protected their borders. He presided over plantations and watched over woodland animals.

He was represented carrying the trunk of a cypress tree. He was also watched over herds, encouraged their fertility and keep wolves at bay. He was depicted or described as an old man, full of good humor, and in love with Pomona.

Sometimes, however, he was represented as an athlete, his head crowned with leaves, holding in one hand a spray of fruit wrapped tightly in an animal skin and in the other, a pruning knife. A sheepdog accompanied him.

On the occasion of sacrifices, which were associated with those of Liber and Pales, the Romans offered him grapes, wheatears, meat, wine and pigs.

Virgil recounts in the *Aeneid* that the ancient Pelasgians, a mythical people that were said to have colonised Greece as well as Italy "dedicated a wood near the city of Cere in Latium to Sylvan, the god of fields and herds and established a feast day in his honor."

Vertumnus

Vertumnus was a divinity believed to be of Etruscan origin, although the etymology remains strictly Latin, and comes from the verb *vertere* meaning "to turn."

The Romans invoked Vertumnus on every occasion involving change: a change of season, a purchase, a sale and the return of floodwaters to their riverbed. Yet, originally, Vertumnus was a divinity that could only watch over the harmonious passage from flower to fruit.

In *The Metamorphoses*, Ovid tells us that Vertumnus was in love with Pomona, and disguised himself or assumed various shapes to seduce her: "Ah! how often, just to see her, he dressed as an old harvester, carrying a basket of wheatears. Often his head crowned

with fresh hay, he was mistaken for a haymaker who had come to cut the grass and turn it in the sun; often, a goad in his hand, one would have said that his sturdy arm had just removed the yoke from tired oxen; weighed down beneath a ladder, he seemed to be on his way to pick fruit. He appeared in turns with the winegrower's pruning knife, a solder's sword or a fisherman's line. Finally, in a thousand different shapes, he tasted the furtive happiness of seeing his beloved."

"One day, wearing a colorful head-dress and leaning on a stick, his temples greying, beneath the features of an old woman, he went into Pomona's orchards. He admired the fruit. 'Such wealth,' he cried; and praising the nymph, he gave her a few kisses, the likes of which no crone has ever given. He sat down, all bent over, on a grassy bank and looked at the trees inclining towards the ground beneath the weight of their fruit."

"Near him, a wide elm held up a vine with long bunches of grapes hanging from it; he praised this happy union: 'If this tree', said he, 'had remained without a companion, it would have only sterile foliage to offer us; if the vine had not married the elm she embraces, we would see her languishing and crawling on the ground."

"But nothing could change Pomona," even though Ovid reprimands her: "And yet, touched by this example, O Pomona, you flee from love, you do not wish to unite with a spouse."

This went on until one day when Vertumnus "weary of these useless disguises, removed the crone's trappings and revealed himself as he was, young and handsome. To Pomona, he appeared like the shimmering image of the sun when it tears apart with its victorious rays a veil of dark clouds that covered it. He wanted to take her by force, but it was useless: the nymph was seized by the god's beauty and her heart was wounded by the same love."

Gardeners offered Vertumnus the first flowers and fruits of their gardens or flowerbeds and adorned his statues with garlands of flower buds.

The Roman people celebrated the feast of Vertumnus on the 23rd of August under the name of *Vertumnalia*, thus giving notice of the change from fine autumn weather to the less pleasant winter season. The importance attached by Rome to the cult of Vertumnus is indicated by the fact that it was presided over by a special priest.

Fertility gods

It was natural that, after imagining divinities to ensure agricultural fecundity, the Romans would invent other gods intended to protect women and ensure their fertility.

Love

The Romans called this god Cupid and he was assimilated to the Greek god Eros. The son of Venus and Mars, he is represented in the arts as a small, winged child who plays tricks on the gods and on mortals to make them fall passionately in love.

His weapons are arrows that he carries in a golden quiver, and sometimes torches that burn anyone who tries to touch them. His arrows are made of gold or lead. Sometimes, Love is represented simply as a child, for he is both the fruit and the symbol of the love between his parents.

Bona Dea

In specifically Roman mythology, Bona Dea or the Good Goddess is a divinity that, depending on the version, is the sister, the wife or the daughter of Faunus, and hence she is sometimes called Fauna. She was honored in Rome as a chaste, prophetic goddess. She revealed her oracle only to women, as Faunus spoke only to men.

Although she was worshipped in a temple on Mount Aventinus, her feast day was celebrated on the 4th of December in the house of the consul or the high magistrate.

The ceremonies were presided over by the Vestal virgins, with no men in attendance, conducted by women bearing flowers who offered a sacrifice of a hog and wine to the Good Goddess. The women became intoxicated by the sound of music and it is probable that the feast ended in an orgy.

In 61 BC, the feast of Bona Dea created a political and religious scandal that tarnished the reputation of Caesar. The anecdote belongs in the category of tragi-comedy. It is told by Plutarch and by Cicero, as well as by Juvenal and Seneca.

Plutarch's version presented in his *Life of Caesar* and summarised in his *Life of Cicero* is the most complete. Its antics are worthy examining and the importance given to the incident demonstrates the degree to which mysterious Oriental divinities prospered in Rome at the end of the Republic.

"Publius Clodius," wrote Plutarch, "was a young patrician, distinguished by his wealth and eloquence, who surpassed in insolence and audacity even the men most famed for their wickedness. He was in love with Pompeia, Caesar's wife. Pompeia was hardly indifferent to him, but her chambers were kept under close surveillance. Aurelia, Caesar's mother, a woman of great virtue, watched over her daughter-in-law so carefully that it was difficult and dangerous for the lovers to meet."

"The Romans have a divinity called the Good Goddess, as the Greeks had their Genecea, the goddess of women. The Phyrigians claim this goddess originated in their country, alleging that she was the mother of King Midas, whereas the Romans pretend that it was a wood nymph who had commerce with the god Faunus. The Greeks maintain that she is the mother of Bacchus who may not be named; hence, they say, the vine branches that cover the women's heads during the feast and the sacred dragon that is said to lie at the feet of the goddess' statue."

"As long as the mysteries last, no man is allowed to enter into the house where they are being celebrated. The women, who withdraw to a separate part of the home, engage in several ceremonies in observance of the Orphic mystery rites. When the time for the feast arrives, the consul or high magistrate whose home has been designated for the celebration, leaves the house with all the other men who dwell there. His wife remains as the mistress of the house and decorates it with appropriate decency. The main ceremonies take place at night, and these evening gatherings are combined with entertainments and concerts."

"One year, Pompeia was celebrating the feast. Clodius, who was still beardless, claimed for that reason no one would recognise him and he presented himself dressed as a woman lyre player. Indeed, he looked very much like a young woman. He found the doors wide open and was introduced without any obstacles by one of Pompeia's slaves, who was in on the secret and went to tell her mistress."

"She was delayed and Clodius did not dare stay where he had been told to wait. He therefore began wandering about the vast dwelling, avoiding the lights, until one of Aurelia's attendants met him. Her eagerness to speak to a person of her sex irritated him and he refused her playful attentions. She dragged him into the middle of the room and demanded to know who he was and where he came from. Clodius replied that he was waiting for Abra (the name of Pompeia's slave), but his voice betrayed him."

"The attendant immediately ran towards the light and the company, crying out that she had just surprised a man in the apartments. The women were seized with fright. Aurelia had all the ceremonies stopped and veiled all the sacred objects. She ordered the doors to be closed and went out carrying flaming torches to search the house."

"She found Clodius in the room of the young girl who had let him in: he was recognised and ignominiously driven out by the women, who left the house in the middle of the night and went to tell their husbands what had happened."

The incident caused an enormous scandal, because Clodius had transgressed the secret of the Bona Dea mystery. To add weight to the charges against him, he was accused of incest with his sister, the wife of Lucullus, the famous gourmet. A trial was held and the accused was absolved. He even had the testimony of Caesar himself in his favor.

It was therefore surprising when, at the same time, Ceasar repudiated Pompeia, who was, after all, suspected of being Clodius' mistress. Caesar is said to have replied with a remark that has since become proverbial: "Caesar"s wife must be above suspicion."

As everything connected to the Good Goddess was secret and hidden, it is difficult to know how she was represented in art. Perhaps it was in the form of a woman holding a newborn in one hand and a suckling pig in the other; it may also have been, in a more obscene way, with manly attributes.

As the Roman conquest of the Mediterranean Basin advanced, the cult of Bona Dea, an authentically Roman goddess, came under the powerful influence of oriental religions and the Mysteries. Other oriental divinities were introduced into the Roman pantheon. There were many of these, but the most famous was Cybele.

Cybele

Cybele was nicknamed "the Mother of the gods" by Ovid in the *Fasti*.

The Latin poet was repeating an expression used by the Greeks of Asia Minor, particularly from Phyrigia, where her cult first began. Why was Cybele given this title? Because Cybele, also known as Rhea, was the wife of Cronos, and consequently, gave birth to the twelve gods of Olympus.

The cult of Cybele was both noisy and wild, and usually involved an orgy. Ovid provides an initial description, again in the *Fasti*: "One would see the procession of mutilated priests (i.e. the eunuchs) go by, beating their drums; the bronze gong would ring beneath the clash of cymbals; the goddess herself, carried on the shoulders of her effeminate ministers, would be paraded through the streets of the city to the shouts of devotees."

The lion was consecrated to her and a team of lions was harnassed to her chariot. In Roman artworks, she was represented on a throne, with her forehead surrounded by a crown of mulberry leaves.

Ovid feigns to ask the Muse Erato: "Why are lions, such ferocious beasts, bending their heads for the first time beneath the yoke, used to pull the goddess' chariot?"

"Cybele softened the fierce ways of men. Her chariot is thus a symbol of her kindness. - But why, Ovid goes on, addressing the Muse of love poetry, does she wear a crenellated crown on her head? Is it because she was the first to give towers to the cities of Phyrigia? A sign from the Muse gave me to understand I had guessed correctly – Where does her fury of self-multilation come from, I asked?"

Erato then recounted the famous, tragic love story of Cybele and Attis: "In the middle of the forest, a Phyrigian child of remarkable beauty named Attis, inspired a chaste passion in the goddess crowned with towers. She wanted to attach him to herself forever and entrust him with guarding her temples.

"Keep forever your child's purity," she told him. Attis promised to obey. "If I do not keep my word," he said, "may my first weakness be my last pleasure."

Nevertheless, he did succumb and ceased to be a child in the arms of the nymph Sangaris. The goddess, irritated, sought revenge. The nymph's tree fell beneath Cybele's blows and the nymph dwelling inside the tree perished with it.

The young Phyrigian lost his mind. Believing that the roof of his home was about to cave in, he fled and went to the highest peaks of Didymus. 'Take away these torches,' he cried, 'take away these whips'. He rent his flesh with a bloody stone and his long hair trailed in the defiled dust."

'That is good, he said. "Let my blood flow to expiate my fault; let that part of me that has caused my misfortune perish'. And before he had finished uttering these words, he struck his lower belly and castrated himself to make every trace of virility disappear."

Lucina

Lucina was held to be a goddess of light and a divinity that brought light to the newborn by watching over their mothers during childbirth. She was often assimilated to Juno who had the same functions.

Ovid addressed her in these terms in the *Fasti*: "O Lucina, it is to you that we owe our vision of the light of day. Tell him: hear the voice of the one calling for your help during the pain of childbirth. May every pregnant woman, with her hair let loose, come and beg Lucina to deliver her gently from the burden she carries in her breast."

Mater Matuta

Mater Matuta was as old as the peoples who lived in Italy in the 9th century, and she embodied dawn and early morning light in her divinity, before becoming the protector of woman and newborn babes who are also at the dawn of their lives.

Her feast was celebrated on the 14th of June, during the festival of the *Matralia*, reserved for married women, who could take part only once by offering cakes to their goddess. She had a temple in Rome on the Forum Boarium, perhaps the one facing the Church of Saint Mary the Egyptian.

Pudicitia

Pudicitia was the divinity who personified the modesty and chastity typical of Roman matrons, who were allowed only one husband during their lifetime.

It should be noted that her cult fell into oblivion at the end of the Roman Empire, when morals were free, except for empresses who sought the protection of this goddess who was represented as a simple woman, without any emblems.

51

The gods
of everyday life

Once the inhabitants of Rome were settled and their city had begun to prosper, they invented divinities capable of overseeing their daily life as well as their dwellings and their health, ensuring their freedom of movement by removing all dangers and assisting them in their final moments during the passage to death.

Abeona and Adeona

Abeona was invoked by those about to leave, whereas those who came back prayed to Adeona.

Aesculapius

Aesculapius, whom the Greeks called Asklepios, was the god of medicine, the son of Apollo and of a priestess.

**The water nymph
Egeria
and Numa Pompilius**

Numa, the successor of Romulus, standing at the right in the painting, comes secretly to a wood to consult Egeria, the water nymph, who would honor him with her love and teach him how to worship the Roman gods.
Nicolas Poussin, 1594-1665.

Aesculapius' entrance into the Roman pantheon is the subject of a legend that Ovid reports in *The Metamorphoses*: "Long ago, a horrible plague infected the air of Latium; blood was corrupted in the veins and people dragged themselves around like living ghosts. Death struck relentlessly, and scoffed at all human efforts and every resource of medical art. They had recourse to the gods."

The Romans went to consult the oracle of Apollo at Delphi, who answered: "It is not Apollo who must put an end to your sufferings, but the son of Apollo. Go under favorable auspices and bring him within your walls."

The Romans went to Epidaurus and "the god appeared to the Romans in a dream, as he is seen in his temples, with a knotty stick in his left hand and his right hand caressing his beard": 'Fear not, I will follow you,' he said to each of them with his friendly voice; but I will change my shape. See this snake wound around my stick; look closely to be sure you recognise it; I will take

his form, but I will be larger, as is fitting when a god shows himself". Transformed into a snake with a golden crest, he embarked on a Roman vessel and landed on the banks of Antium in Italy.

The god unrolled his huge rings as he slithered into the temple of Apollo, erected on the shores…Then he made a furrow across the sand with his burning scales, climbed the length of the rudder and once again laid his head against the stern."

"The ship travelled all the way to the mouth of the Tiber. There, an entire people, and the men, women and sacred virgins of Vesta, hurried to meet the god: a thousand cries of joy greeted his coming. As the ship quickly sailed up the river waters, incense burned and crackled on altars raised along the riverbanks; clouds of fragrance rose into the air; victims fell beneath the smoking iron of sacrifice. Finally, they arrived at the capital of the universe: the serpent climbed to the very top of the mast; he shook his head and looked around him to decide where he would dwell. The Tiber, in its

course, divides into two branches of equal width, and their waters surround an island, which bears the name of the river. It is there that the snake decided to repair, once he had left the ship; he recovered his normal aspect, put an end to the plague and his presence saved Rome."

Alemona

Alemona was present every time the Romans went past or through a door.

Carna

Carna whose name was attached to that of caro or flesh, oversaw the physical well being of human beings, especially the proper functioning of the heart.

According to Ovid in the *Fasti*, she was also "the goddess of hinges; she opens what is shut, and shuts what is open; those are the attributes of her divinity. Whence comes this power?

The answer seems to lie hidden by the mists of time, but all doubt shall be dissipated by my verses. Not far from the edge of the Tiber there stood an ancient wood, where the priests still go today to offer sacrifices. There was born a nymph named Grane by our ancestors.

Many lovers vied for her favors but she had refused them all. She went about the countryside, hunting wild beasts, her javelin in her hand, or stretching the knotty mesh of her nets at the entrance to deep valleys. She did not wear a quiver; yet she was mistaken for the sister of Phoebus.

If some young lover addressed her with passionate words, she immediately replied: 'There is too much daylight here and daytime plays a great role in modesty; take me to a remote cave, I will follow you'. The credulous lover would penetrate into the depths of a lair; the nymph came upon some bushes, stopped and hid within them. Janus saw her; at the sight of her, he was filled with fiery passion: he tried to soften the heart of this inflexible beauty with sweet words; the nymph, as was her custom, asked him to find a solitary refuge; she pretended to follow and accompany him, but soon the guide found himself alone; he had just been abandoned. But it was in vain, O demented nymph! Janus already knows where you are hiding. It is in vain, I say, for below the rock where you have taken refuge, he holds you tightly in his arms, possesses you and cries: "For the price of your favors, for the price of your lost virginity, I shall put hinges under your power'. And at these words, he gave her a branch of hawthorn, to brush away from doors any harmful adventure."

Ovid tells another story about her which depicts her as the protectress of the household, driving away the strygia that suck, like vampires, the blood of newborn babes, by sprinkling water with powerful virtues on the threshold, and "holding in her hand the raw entrails of a two-month-old sow:

'Spare,' she says, "birds of the night, the entrails of this child; that a different victim, equally young, shall replace the young child; take, I beg you, heart for heart, fibre for fibre; we abandon this existence to you to save another, more precious one."

The feast of Carna was celebrated on the 1st of June. Ovid tells us that on that day a suckling pig was killed and it was eaten with beans mixed with flour; this stew was thought to protect against bellyaches.

Cura

Cura oversaw the countries visited by souls after death.

Aesculapius

He is carrying his main attribute, a club with a snake wound around it, the famous caduceus of our physicians, as he is their protector and colleague. He is wearing a small traveller's hat on his head, as he often took journeys to visit his patients. Marble, Roman period.

Egeria

Egeria, one of the prophetic nymphs of Roman mythology, had a secret relationship in woods and caves with King Numa, and it was said that she became his second wife. In *The Metamorphoses*, Ovid recounts that at the death of Numa "the nymph Egeria, went away from Rome and hid her sorrow in the dark forests of Aricia (a town in Latium) where she disturbed the cult of Diana with her moaning and lamentations. Hippolytus, the son of Theseus, went to visit her and tried to console her by evoking his own misfortunes, which in her view were not comparable to hers, but it was in vain."

"Lying sorrowfully at the foot of Mount Albanus, Egeria wept. Finally, Apollo's sister Diana, touched by the sight of her pious grief, turned the nymph into a spring that would never run dry."

Febris

Febris is a divinity whose role was to lower the fever of those afflicted with it.

Fornax

Fornax was in charge of overseeing the proper baking of bread, the staple of the ancient Roman diet, in the baker's oven. The festival of the *Fornacalia* was celebrated on the 17th of February.

Juturna

Juturna, a mere water nymph of Latium, was famous for her miraculous cures and her water that was used at sacrifices.

She was immortalized by Jupiter who had loved her under circumstances recounted by Ovid in the *Fasti:* "Jupiter, seized with a violent passion for the nymph Juturna, was treated to great disdain, such as a powerful god could hardly expect. Sometimes she would hide in the forests among the hazel trees, and sometimes she took refuge in the waters that acknowledged her as their sovereign."

Jupiter succeeded in seducing her, and to thank her for yielding to him, he made her a divinity of waters and good health. In Rome, a pond inside the Forum, between the temple of Castor and Vesta, was given the name Lake Juturna, and a temple was built on the Field of Mars not far from the aqueduct.

Virgil sang of her in the *Aeneid*. She was, indeed, the sister of King Turnus, who fought Aeneas. "Juturna presided over the lakes and bubbling rivers; Jupiter, the

all-powerful king of the heavens, had granted her this sacred empire as the price of her virginity which he stole from her.

Juno asked her to protect her brother against the machinations of Aeneas in these terms: "Nymph, the ornament of the rivers, you who are dear to my heart, you know that of all the Latin virgins who entered the unfaithful bed of great Jupiter, you are the only one I have distinguished by my goodness, the only one to whom I have given a place among the celestial dwellings. If you can attempt some great stroke on behalf of your brother, you must dare to do it, for it is your duty."

Despite Juturna's efforts, Turnus was to perish at the hands of Aeneas. Her feast day was celebrated by the hydraulic engineers' guild on the 11th of January, and she was naturally invoked whenever Rome was ravaged by one of many fires.

Larves

Larves have a certain kinship with Lemures and Lares, but they also have their own specific features: they embody the souls of the dead who have committed crimes or who were murdered, and they come back to earth to haunt those who had a connection to these rather cursed souls.

In Hell, they continue their evil actions by tormenting the unfortunate souls delivered over to them.

Lemures

Like Lares and Larves, Lemures embody the spirits of the dead. Lemures were thought to spend the night wandering so as to torment the living.

Libitina

Libitina was worshipped in a temple in Rome that contained all the objects required to organise a funeral procession. She oversaw compliance with funerary rituals. She ended up being assimilated to death itself.

Luna

Luna, the goddess of the moon, came much earlier in the Roman pantheon than the Greek Selena or Diana, with whom she was confused.

Luna answered to the evocative surname of Noctiluca, the light of the night, to such an extent that symbolically, a lamp remained lighted all night in her temple on Mount Palatine in Rome.

Parcae

The Parcae or Fates were called Moirai in ancient Greece.

There were three of these divinities of birth and death, who spent their time spinning human destinies: Clotho, whose attribute was a spindle, Lachesis whose attribute was a measuring stick with which she made marks on a globe, and Atropos, whose attribute was a sun dial (or perhaps a pair of scissors to cut the thread of life).

Portunus

Portunus (or Ino) was a spirit who protected harbors. Her festival was the Portunalia on the 17th of August.

During these ceremonies, keys were thrown into the fire as a tribute to the divinity whowas often represented as a young man carrying keys.

Salacia

Salacia was the goddess of the sea and one of the wives of Neptune. The etymology of her name is telling: it refers to the sal, the salty wave, and consequently designates the vast, high seas.

Salus

Salus was a Roman divinity, a personified abstraction of safety, namely health, prosperity and public well being, in other words, the proper functioning of the administration of Roman citizens.

A temple was built in her honor on the Quirinal in Rome starting in the 4th century BC and she was worshipped on the 30th of April, the same day devoted to Peace, Concord and Janus.

She was represented under the appearance of a woman at the helm, with a globe at her feet, or sometimes as a seated woman pouring a libation into a patera on an altar, wound round by a snake, like the Greek goddess Hygieia to whom she was assimilated.

Somnus

Somnus, the personification of sleep, was depicted as the brother of Death, the son of Night, along with Morpheus, to whom he ended up being assimilated.

Somnus was associated with sleep-inducing potions made of poppies and calming beverages flowing from a horn.

Detail of a mask of the statue of Thalia

This theatre mask may represent one of the terrifying nocturnal divinities such as Larves or Lemures, the divinities of nightmares who sought to frighten the living.
Greek marble, Roman period

State divinities

The Roman state placed itself under the protection of a number of divinities that enabled it to assume its duties and defend itself against outside enemies.

Aeternitas

Aeternitas was of crucial importance to Roman ideology. Indeed, she personified not only Eternity in general, but also that of Rome in particular, and later on, of the Roman Empire. This divinity was often represented on imperial coins as a woman with a stern countenance, surrounded by various symbolic attributes.

These symbols included a sphere covered with stars on which she was seated, or which lay underfoot, a snake biting its tail, a ring as the emblem of that which has neither beginning nor end, a phoenix rising from its ashes, holding in its hands either the sun and the moon, the eternal planets, or a sceptre and a cornucopia.

Aius Locutius

Aius Locutius was a divinity born of History. The Romans invented him when the Gauls marched on Rome in 390 BC. Indeed, in the stillness of the night a voice was heard announcing their approach, but no one paid any attention to it.

After the city was stormed and set on fire by the Gauls, when the Romans rebuilt their sanctuaries, they remembered the voice they had ignored. To expiate their indifference, they erected an altar in honor of the god, who was given the name Aius Locutius or Loquens, in other words, the Prophetic Speaker.

Anna Perenna

According to Ovid and Virgil, Anna Perenna was the sister of Dido who, suffering from unrequited love of Aeneas, had herself burnt at the stake. After Dido's death, Anna fled to Carthage in Italy, where she was received kindly by Aeneas. She had the unfortunate idea of arousing the jealousy of Lavinia, Aeneas' wife, and when Dido warned her of impending danger in a dream, she ran away, only to drown in the Nimicius, a small river in Latium on the shores of which Aeneas himself would one day be buried.

Ovid also tells us that Anna Perenna was an old woman who busied herself with feeding the plebeians when they revolted against the patricians and withdrew to Mount Aventine. As a sign of gratitude, the plebeians erected a temple in her name. Ovid also recounts in the *Fasti* that Anna "had just been ranked among the goddesses. Mars came and drew her aside, speaking in these terms: 'Your feast day falls during the month that belongs to me; your cult and mine are joined; do not refuse to serve me; you can have a far-reaching effect on my happiness. I, the god of war, long for Minerva, the goddess of war; for a long time now my heart has suffered from this wound; do whatever is in your power to join together in a single god these two divinities that already have so much in common; it is a perfect role for you, good and zealous Anna."

"He spoke; the old woman beguiled him with a deceitful promise, and putting him off day after day, nourished his naïve hope for a long time. Finally, the impatient god grew more insistent: 'Your wishes shall be accomplished,' she told him; 'vanquished with difficulty through my prayers, she has finally consented.' The lover surrendered to his joy and prepared the marriage bed; Anna allowed herself to be led to him, her face veiled like a young wife. As he was about to cover her with kisses, Mars recognised her. The confused god was shaken, first by shame, then by anger. The new goddess mocked Mars' passion for beautiful Minerva, and Venus never laughed so heartily. That is the origin of the obscene jokes and chants. It is to celebrate the hoax played on a powerful god."

She was held to be the goddess who protected the yearly cycle and her feast took place during the full moon of the first month of the Roman year, in other words, on the Ides of March, the 15th of March, in a wood at the edge of the Tiber. Ovid described the feast in these terms in the *Fasti*: "Everyone drinks as much as he wishes, stretched out in the grass beside his beloved. Some remain in the open air, others put up tents or huts of branches and leaves. Still others drive wooden pickets into the ground to suspend their clothes. The sun and the wine warm their senses. They empty their cup to the health of years past and those to come. People sing well-known melodies from theatre repertoires. They dance and the beloved lets her hair float in the wind. At the end of the festivities, they all stagger home. A drunken old man is led on by a drunken woman."

Fides

Fides or Good Faith was one of the Roman divinities that came under the category of an abstraction, designed to promote faith in the destiny of Rome. Her feast day was celebrated on the 1st of October and she was represented on coins in the form of a goddess with various attributes, such as wheatears, fruit, a globe, a cornucopia, victory, an eagle or a standard.

The Camenae

The Camenae were prophetic nymphs (*cano*, I predict in verse) derived from the very ancient Italic religion. They have been assimilated somewhat to the Greek Muses.

The most important one was Carmenta, the goddess of Destiny and Fortune, who knew both past and future. She was venerated in a temple at the foot of Mount Capitoline, and at altars near the gate known as the Carmentalia. She was sometimes said to be the assistant of Lucina and Candelifera who presided over childbirth.

Concordia

Concordia, the goddess Concord, personified harmony and peace. Several temples were dedicated to her in Rome. She was represented on coins as a Roman matron, either seated or standing, holding a cornucopia in her left hand and an olive branch in her right hand. Her feast was celebrated on the 16th of January and on the 30th of March.

Evander

Some sixty years before the Trojan War, Evander or Evandrus led a colony from Pallanteum in Arcadia to Italy, where he built the city of Pallanteum on the banks of the Tiber River at the foot of Mount Palatine, the site of the future city of Rome.

Evander taught his neighbors new laws that were gentler than the old ones, along with the arts of peace and social life, writing and the existence of the twelve gods of Olympus.

Fortuna

Fortuna or Fortune, an all-important divinity in ancient Roman beliefs, was the goddess of changeable Destiny. She was symbolised by the wheel of Fortune, but she also carried certain attributes such as a ball representing the fickleness of Fortune, a cornucopia, and a baton with which she guided and conducted the world's affairs. Her feast day took place in Antium and Preneste on the 24th of June, the summer solstice, and her oracles were famous and received with great attention by all those who wished to know their future and the fate of the world. At the end of the *Fasti*, Ovid salutes her in these words: "And it is already time for another festival of Fortuna. It has come back again so quickly! Just seven more days, and June will be over. Go out, ye Romans, and joyfully honor the goddess Fortuna; her temple, on the Tiber River, is the gift of a king. Cross the bridges on foot or take a swift boat over the waters and do not be ashamed of returning to your dwelling in a drunken state. Let the skiffs crowned with flowers carry the feasts and the young guests; and let the wine be drunk in long draughts on the water's surface. The people celebrate this goddess because, it is said, the founder of her temple was a plebeian who rose from his humble condition to the throne of the kings. This feast day is also cherished by slaves because the man who dedicated this temple to the fickle divinity that stands next to our walls was the Roman King Tullius, the son of a slave woman."

Honos

Honos, the personification of military honor, was represented with the features of a young warrior carrying a spear and a goat's horn. He was adored in Rome where many temples were erected in his name, including one that faced the temple of the goddess Virtue, or Courage, and his cult is often associated with hers.

Janus and Jana

Janus and Jana, an ancient couple of Latin divinities, were adored as the image of the sun and the moon. The names of Janus and Jana were doubtless derived from Dianus and Diana, terms that had the same root – *dies*, meaning "day." Janus occupied a singularly important place in Roman religion.

Ovid drew a lyrical portrait of him and his attributes in the *Fasti*, in the form of a vision: "O double-faced god, it is from you that the year begins to run its silent course; you, who without turning your head, sees what no other god can see, be favorable to the leaders whose active solicitude brings rest to the Ocean and safety to the land that lavishes its treasures upon us; bestow favor upon your senators, the people of Quirinus and with a sign, open unto us the doors of your sanctuary. […]"

"But how shall I speak of you, twin-faced Janus? Greece has no divinity that resembles you. Tell us why, then, alone among the immortals, you see what lies before you and what lies behind. While I, with my tablets, turned these questions around in my head, a brilliant light spread throughout my dwelling and suddenly there appeared before me the holy, the marvellous double-faced Janus!"

"Holding a stick in his right hand, and a key in his left, the god called out these words to me: 'Once, long ago, I was called Chaos. The diaphanous air and the other elements – fire, water and earth – held together and made a single world; but these ill-sorted natures could not remain united for long and they broke their bonds and disseminated into space. Fire rose to the higher regions, below was the realm of air, and in between settled earth and water. It is there that I ceased to be a rough, shapeless mass and took the form and face of a god. Even now I still bear a few traces of that primitive confusion; I am the same in front and behind; but there is another reason for my singular appearance; in telling you, I shall teach you wherein my power lies."

"Everything my eyes can encompass – the skies, the Ocean, the clouds and the earth – to my hand has been given the power to open and close them; I have been entrusted with guarding this vast universe; I am the one who makes it turn on its hinges. [...] Now that you know my power, I shall explain my face to you. [...]"

"Every door has two sides, one looking out onto the street and the other at the household god; seated near the threshold of your home, the doorkeeper sees people go in and out: as the doorkeeper of the home of the gods, my eyes look upon the East and the West... For fear that in turning my head I might lose precious moments, it has been given to me to see in front and behind at the same time, without moving."

Ovid asks Janus a series of questions, including this one: "Why, when offering sacrifices to other gods, must I begin by offering both incense and wine to you?" – "So that, as the guardian of the celestial dwellings, I shall allow your prayers easy access to each divinity." – "Why do we exchange wishes of happiness and kind words on the day of your Calends?" – "There is an omen," he said, leaning on the stick he held in his right hand, "connected to the beginning of all things; the first word is listened to with fearful attention; the first bird to appear is the one that determines the augur. The temples have just opened, the gods lend their ears; not a single prayer uttered from the mouth of mortals is lost, every syllable resounds in the heavens."

Thus, Janus presided over the beginning of all things and he was always invoked at the start of an enterprise, even before Jupiter. He opened the year and the seasons, to such an extent that the first month of the year bears the name of Janus, Januarus, January. He was also the gatekeeper of the heavens and in that capacity received a number of nicknames, such as The Opener and The Closer. On earth, he was the essential divinity, the guardian of keys and doors, and he was represented with two heads because every door faces in two directions (Janus *bifrons*). Occasionally he was represented with four heads, and as such, was the god of the four seasons.

In wartime, the temples of Janus in Rome, like the one in Bellone, were left open to express symbolically that the god had gone out to the battlefield to help the Roman warriors. On the other hand, as soon as peace returned, Janus went back to his temple and the doors were closed again so that the god who held the city in his safekeeping, would not go away. On the first day of the new year, the feast of Janus, Romans gave each other gifts of sweets and copper coins representing two-headed Janus on one side, and a ship on the other. These gifts were called *strenae*.

Janus was given a different, much more earthly origin by Macrobius in the *Saturnalia*. The writer, who was following ancestral Latin traditions, claimed that "Janus reigned over the country that we now call Italy. [...] Janus is believed to have two faces, in order to see what is happening in front of him and behind him, which must be interpreted as the caution and skill of the king, who knew the past and predicted the future. [...] Yet Janus, after offering hospitality to Saturn who arrived in the country by ship, learned from his guest the art of agriculture and of perfecting foods that were rough and wild until he learned how to produce them from the earth, and shared his crown with Saturn. Janus was also the first to strike copper coins; and he demonstrated such respect for Saturn in this institution that he had one side struck with a ship because Saturn had arrived on a ship, and on the other, the effigy of the god's head, to hand down his memory to posterity. [...] It is generally held that Saturn and Janus ruled together in peace and that they built jointly two neighboring cities in the same region, which is confirmed by the testimony of Virgil who said: 'One was named Janiculum and the other Saturnalia."

Libertas

Libertas or Liberty was one of the numerous political and moral entities that became divinized. She was the guarantor of freedoms in the Roman Republic and in its Constitution. On her head, she wore a *pileus*, the round bonnet of the freemen, and carried a sceptre and spear, sometimes with an olive branch. Sometimes she was crowned with a diadem and held the bonnet in her hand. Her cult was often associated with that of Jupiter.

Majestas

Majesta or Majesty, was also a divinized entity in the Roman pantheon. She was constantly invoked as a sign of the respect due to Rome and the Roman people. Failure to perform one's duty as a citizen was a crime against the Majesty of Rome, one of the worst possible, and was often punished by death.

Moneta

Moneta or Money was originally an Italiot divinity in her own right, before becoming one of the nicknames of Juno. As the etymology indicates, she was the protector of currency and of the prosperity that flowed from it. Her temple was situated on the Capitol and also served as the mint.

Necessitas

Necessitas or Necessity personified fatality, the immutable laws of nature that are required to hold the world together. Her power was such that both men and gods were compelled to bend to her wishes. She was represented in the form of a tall woman holding bronze nails, which she used to fix the decrees of fate.

Pax

Pax is the goddess of Peace, acknowledged as such under the reign of Emperor Augustus, in homage to his government based on the Pax Romana throughout the world. Her altar was built on the Field of Mars in the year 9 BC and a temple was erected for her cult under Emperor Vespasian in 75 AD. She is represented as a young Roman woman carrying a cornucopia and an olive branch. Her feast day was the 3rd of January.

Providentia

As her name suggests, Providentia was the goddess who watched over anyone who accomplished the destiny of Rome. Hence, this divinity was associated with Roman emperors and the reigning titleholder. She was represented on coins as a woman with a sceptre, a globe and a cornucopia in her hand.

Spes

Spes, the personification of Hope, was honored in Rome, where several temples were built in her name.

Suada

Suada or Suadela was the goddess of Persuasion.

Terminus

Terminus was a Roman god who presided over limits and boundaries. His cult was political. It was instituted by King Numa, the great lawmaker of ancient Rome. Indeed, the sovereign ordered all Romans to put markers around their rural property dedicated to Jupiter and offered sacrifices every year to these boundary stones on the feast of the Terminalia in honor of Terminus of the 23rd of February.

The cult of Terminus has been described at length by Ovid in the *Fasti*: "O Terminus, whether we worship you in the form of a block of stone or an old tree trunk torn from the earth, you remain a god. The masters of two adjacent fields crown you at the same time; they offer you two garlands and two sacred cakes. An altar is set up; the ploughman's wife goes off to get fire from her hearth and carries a few burning coals in a roasting dish; an old man splits wooden logs and with great difficulty drives posts into the stone that resists, where the bonfire is set." "While he lights the first fire with dry bark, a child is beside him, holding in his hands a large basket, and when he has thrown wheat three times into the flames, his younger sister presents a slice of honeycomb taken from the hive; others carry wine for libations, which is poured from each cup onto the fire; the crowd of attendants, dressed in white, keep a religious silence. The blood of a lamb reddens the statue of the common god Terminus; he is not offended if a suckling sow is substituted for the lamb. However, all the neighbors have gathered and sit down together around a table where rustic merrymaking prevails; and then they celebrate your kindness, inviolable Terminus. You serve as a boundary between peoples, cities and kingdoms; without you, the smallest corner of the earth would give rise to endless quarreling. Impartial among all, and incorruptible, you are the safe and sure guardian of the

Roman roads

This road, once deeply rutted by passing carts, wagons and chariots, is an apt symbol of the many activities of the Roman State. It was by these roads that the divinities imported by Roman religion were first introduced.

fields that have been entrusted to you." A similar festival for the god Terminus of the Roman State was originally held between the fifth and sixth milestones on the road to Laurentum, near a place called Festi.

Another Terminus festival, also public, took place near the temple of Jupiter at the Capitol. This indicates how important he was in a state governed by the rule of law, where legislation played such an important role that his cult lasted a long time and neighboring peoples took up the practice of making a sacrifice and sharing a meal together.

Victoria

Victoria is the goddess who, as her name indicates, enabled Rome to vanquish its enemies. She was a very ancient, purely Roman divinity, dating back to a period well before the Romanized version of the Greek pantheon and her assimilation to Nike. Before coming under Roman domination, the Sabines worshipped a goddess named Vacuna, the protector or fields and woods, as well as a warrior, who was gradually assimilated to Victoria. Similarly, the Latins in Latium worshipped Victoria Pota, a goddess who symbolised victory and power.

Soon, a statue of the goddess Victoria was raised in Rome, the conqueror of the entire Mediterranean Basin. The Roman commanders-in-chief showed great respect for her cult, and one of them, Sulla, dedicated Games to her in the 1st century BC. Caesar had an altar erected in her honor in the Senate assembly hall and demanded that an oath of loyalty to the Empire be sworn there on the 28th of August. Later on, after Augustus claimed victory over Cleopatra and Mark Anthony at Actium in 31 BC, he placed Rome under the protection of Victoria. A temple was built for devotions to her on Mount Palatine. At ceremonies and processions in honor of the emperor, it was customary to parade a statue of Victory, who ended up being known as the Emperor's Companion. Victoria was honored in all the large cities of the empire. In Roman Gaul, she adorned the great altar of the Three Gauls at the top of Fourvière hill.

There was no imperial cult that did not include Victoria as the emblem and symbol of lasting, eternally victorious empire. The coins on which she was represented show her on the back of the emperor's effigy, bare-breasted, holding a crown of laurel leaves. In statuary she is portrayed with wings, like the Winged Victory of Samothrace.

Procession of Ara Pacis Augustae

Roman religion was a state religion in which the priests were civil servants and the faithful the entire Roman people, including children, who took part in the procession.
Roman marble, 1st century

Following pages
Victory

For a city that claimed to rule the world, Victory was an immensely important goddess. In her winged form, she flew to the side of the Romans in battle and protected them against their adversaries.
Roman replica of a Hellenistic bas-relief of marble.

Pages 68-69
Palmyra

These Roman temples that defy the ages testify to the universal power of Roman religion and its ambition to dominate the conquered Orient. Here, a set of four columns that indicated a major crossroads, served no other purpose than "architectural stylishness".

GRECO-ROMAN GODS

As Rome became a Mediterranean and world power, conquering numerous territories formerly under the domination and jurisdiction of the Greeks, Greek divinities gradually joined the national gods derived from the very ancient pantheons of the peoples that founded Rome.

Many of the Greek gods and goddesses enjoyed the same powers and influence as divinities in the Roman pantheon, and hence came to be associated with them, as well as with their attributes and attributions. Indeed, the Romans were a very tolerant people in religious matters, and they were quick to include foreign divinities in their cults and devotions and transform them into Roman gods.

This tolerance does not mean that the Romans merely reproduced the Greek divinities and that their own gods and goddesses lost their particular characteristics or individual identity. Roman writers, especially the poets, were eager to introduce the twelve gods of the Olympian pantheon in Greece into a mythology that endeavored to remain specifically Roman. In short, the great gods of Rome were not copies or clones of their Greek predecessors, as is all too often presumed to be the case. Nevertheless, for purposes of clarity and to indicate the differences, we will always mention to which Greek divinity a Roman divinity corresponds, and in this chapter, we have classified them in order of importance rather than in alphabetical order.

Jupiter

The sovereign of all the gods was Jupiter (Zeus). Like his Greek counterpart, his emblem was the eagle and his attributes a sceptre and lightning. A Roman legend of his birth, based on the Greek, is recounted by Ovid in the *Fasti*:

"It was said that the nymph Amaltheia, noble daughter of the Cretan Ida, hid Jupiter deep in the forest. She had a she-goat, mother of two kids, who was known for her beauty among all the herds in Crete; the goat had raised horns that curled over her back and she was worthy of nourishing the great Jupiter. She suckled the god; but one day the goat's horns broke against a tree and she lost half of her adornment."

Amaltheia picked up the broken horn, surrounded it with fresh herbs, filled it with fruit and presented it thus to the lips of Jupiter. When the god reigned in the heavens, seated on the throne of his father (Cronos), when Jupiter, by his victory, had everything at his feet, he gave the she-goat and her fertile horn (the famous horn of plenty) the rank of stars."

Jupiter existed well before the Romans learned about the Greek gods through conquest and culture. He was a god of the elements called Dovis Pater, a name that was contracted to Diospiter, signifying "father" or "master of the sky."

The Romans, who were always practical, worshipped him in this capacity as the god of rain, wind, thunder and lightning, which had beneficial or harmful effects on agriculture. To designate him as such, the Romans gave him nicknames with obvious meanings that hardly need translation such as *Pluvius*, *Fulgurator*, *Tonitrualis*, *Tonans* and *Fulminator*.

As he had pre-eminence over all the other gods, the Romans gave him the title of *Optimus*, *Maximus*, in other words, the Good and the Great. His temple stood in Rome on the rugged Capitoline Hill at the edge of the Tarpeian Rock, prompting the Romans, who were always very fussy about the designations of their gods, to give him the patronymics of Capitolinus and Tarpeius.

Throne
of a priest of Bacchus
This throne, with its winged lions harnessed to the chariot of Bacchus-Dionysus, is, in its oriental and Hellenic richness, the fruit of a meeting of two mythologies, Greek and Roman.

Jupiter was considered the prime protector of Rome, and in this capacity, he played a political role, which the two consuls who assumed their duties each year acknowledged by officially worshipping him. Similarly, when victorious generals returned to Rome in triumph, they always made a solemn procession along the Appian Way to the temple of Jupiter to perform acts of thanksgiving.

As a result, Jupiter was the supreme head of the Roman armies and the commanders-in-chief were merely his representatives.

He was designated at the time by the laudatory epithets of *Imperator*, the Commander-in-chief, *Victor*, the Victorious, *Invictus*, the Invincible, *Stator*, the Guardian-Founder, *Opitulus*, the Helpful, *Feretrius*, the Conqueror, *Praedator*, the Lover of Spoils, *Triumphator*, the Triumphant, and many others.

Since Jupiter had a temple in Rome under each of these names, it is easy enough to imagine how many there must have been.

Just as he presided over the great Roman Games under the invocation of Jupiter Capitolinus, he was invoked as Jupiter Latialis as the patron of the Latin festival. More than for the Greeks, he was the god who determined the destiny of humanity, and imposed his sovereign will upon events.

He also revealed the future of men, through his priests known as augurs, who read messages from Jupiter in the many signs beheld in the sky, especially in the flight of birds. Similarly, he was called *Prodigalis*, because he called forth miracles upon the earth, as lucky or unlucky signs.

Whenever the Romans made a decision about sacred or profane matters, they invoked Jupiter because the god of gods was the source of all human activities. As guardian of the laws and protector of justice, he watched over sacred compliance with oaths and presided over political debates and trials. In his capacity as ruler of the sky and prince of light, the color white was dedicated to him and white animals, cows or sheep, were sacrificed to him.

According to the mythology, Jupiter always traveled in a chariot pulled by four white horses, and his priest, the Flamines dialis, the first in the hierarchy of servants of the Roman gods, responsible for serving their numerous cults, wore white caps. Consuls wore white garments when they offered sacrifices to Jupiter on the day they took office, the first day of January.

It is true that the Romans adopted all the legends circulating in Greece concerning Jupiter, especially about his loves.

In this regard, Ovid recounts in *The Metamorphoses* one of the ways in which Jupiter exercised his seductive talents.

One day, he addressed Mercury in these terms: "Trusty minister of my commands," he said, "[…] speed your course and descend to earth […]. There you shall find a royal herd grazing. Lead them to the shore."

No sooner had he spoken when already the bulls, driven from the hills, moved, according to Jupiter's will, towards the water's edge where Europa, daughter of the powerful king of the country (Agenor), was sporting with her companions, the virgins of Tyr. Love ill agrees with kingly majesty; setting aside the dignity of empire, the master of the gods […] Jupiter assumed the form of a bull. […] He bellowed and wandered over the plains in his graceful form. His skin was whiter than snow that has not been sullied by traveller's steps, nor softened by the humid breath of southern skies; his neck was straight and muscular, and his dewlap hung in long folds upon his breast; his horns were small but seemed polished brighter than a diamond by a craftsman's hand; his forehead bore no threat, his eyes were peaceful; softness reigned in every feature."

"Delighted by his beauty, Agenor's daughter was surprised at his gentleness; yet despite his softness, she dared not touch him; soon she came up to him and fed flowers to his ivory-colored mouth. Her lover started with joy; awaiting the happiness he sought, he kissed the hands of Europa. Ah! He could barely confine the pleasures of impatience, playing and bounding across the green grass, or lying down and rolling his white flanks against the golden sand."

"Slowly reassured, Europa stroked the breast he presented for the caresses of her pure hand and wound garlands of flowers around his horns. Finally, Agenor's daughter, not knowing who he was, dared to mount upon his back. The god then rode over field and arid meadow to the shore, where he dipped his hoofs and wet his thighs, then plunged in and carried off his prize. Europa, trembling, yielded to him and turned her gaze to the now distant shore; her right hand grasped the bull's horn, the left pressed against his back, and the waving folds of her gown swelled and floated in the wind."

Jupiter

Endowed with dignity, physical strength and wisdom, Jupiter perfectly embodied the king of the gods, but he was also close to the Romans, for he was represented wearing a toga, with a panel thrown over his shoulder. Roman bronze from Asia Minor, 1st-2nd centuries.

Juno

Juno was the wife of Jupiter, just as Hera was the wife of Zeus in Greek mythology. She was also his sister, as Ovid explains in the *Fasti*: "It is something to have wed Jupiter, to be his sister. I don't know whether I should be prouder that he is my brother or that he is my husband." The month of June is dedicated to her and in the *Fasti*, Ovid has the goddess declare: "I am worshipped at a hundred altars, but there is no honor I prefer to that of giving my name to this month; I have received this honor not only in Rome, but the neighboring peoples have shown me the same deference."

In early Rome, she went by the name of Regina or Queen, testifying to her supremacy over all the other goddesses and the heavens, which she governed along with her husband. Jupiter was assigned the task of protecting men, whereas Juno's function was to look after women, for whom she stood as the primary model. Like a sort of guardian angel, she was thought to accompany every woman throughout her life, from birth to death. Roman women offered sacrifices to her on their birthday, calling her Juno Natalis. Consequently, the goddess also had nicknames, like her husband Jupiter, to describe each of her attributions. She was called *Virginalis* or the Virginal, and *Matrona* or the Matron, in other words, a woman who has had children. She was also given other epithets such as *Opigena* or the Helper, as she assisted women in childbirth, and *Sospita*, the Liberator.

The greatest feast day dedicated to Juno was the *Matronalia*, which was held on the first day of March. Since she formed a couple with Jupiter, she was considered the goddess of the marriage of women, which earned her the description of *Juga* or *Jugalis*, the Conjugal, and *Pronuba*, who presided over weddings and *Cinxia*, protector of nuptials. When women gave birth, they called out to Juno Licinia for help, and their newborn children were also placed under her protection. Juno gave her name to the month of June, held to be the best month for marrying. She also had many other unexpected powers.

The Roman State considered her the guardian of finances, no doubt because she held the purse strings in the family, overseeing expenditures and savings. A temple was erected in her honor on Mount Capitoline where treasury coins were kept, designating her by the name of Moneta.

Minerva

Minerva, assimilated to the Greek goddess Athena, also known as Pallas, has a telling Latin etymology since her name is derived from the root *mens* or mind. Indeed, for the Romans she personified the power of thought.

She shared her sanctuary on the Capitoline Hill with Jupiter and Juno.

There was another temple dedicated to her on the Aventine, as well as at the foot of Mount Coelius where she went by the nickname *Capta*. In short, in the hierarchy of the twelve most important divinities, she ranked third, alongside the two most powerful gods.

The Romans honored her as the goddess of wisdom and the protector of the arts and poetry, and the trades, especially the household arts.

In this regard, Ovid emphasises in the *Fasti* that she taught "the art of softening wool, filling the distaffs and spinning them [...] of making the shuttle fly across yarns held fast on the loom and tightening the loose weft with the ivory comb."

Ovid calls out to members of various professions, placing them under the protection of Minerva: "Masters, even deprived of wages, never cease to respect the goddess who will bring you new employees. And you who know how to engrave, you enamelers who paint with brilliant colors, you whose clever chisel gives marble voluptuous contours, there is no form of work over which Minerva does not preside."

She also guided warriors through the dangers of war with her caution, courage and perseverance, three qualities that would ensure victory. Under this attribution, she was represented with a helmet, a shield and a coat of mail. To thank her for helping to achieve victory, Roman soldiers dedicated part of the spoils taken from the enemy to her.

Minerva was a goddess who presented many faces, since the Romans also worshipped her in her capacity as the creator of musical instruments that had an important role in religious and ritual ceremonies.

During the final days of the festival dedicated to her between the 19th and 23rd of March known as the *Quinquatrus*, it was thus customary to invoke her help and protection to purify trumpets, lyres, harps and various drums and timpani.

Her attributes were the owl, the shield and the olive branch.

Minerva

According to tradition, Minerva (Athena for the Greeks) wore the helmet of a warrior goddess and a breastplate bearing the head of Medusa.
Oriental alabaster,
Imperial Roman era.

Bacchus

Bacchus, the Roman counterpart of the Greek god Dionysus, was sometimes assimilated to Liber, one of the Roman fertility gods.

He was worshipped by the offering of honey cakes, for he had discovered honey.

A woman gave him the cakes, for, Ovid tells us in the *Fasti*, Bacchus led choruses of women, his thyrsus in hand. The woman was old,

Ovid continues, because at that age one enjoys wine and Bacchus "has a weakness for the gifts of the fertile vine."

The woman was crowned with ivy because it was a plant that Bacchus cherished. Ovid observed that children received the free toga on the feast day, because it combined "the grace of youth and that of childhood, and also because, under the name of Liber, it expresses the freedom of the toga in all its auspices."

Apollo

Apollo went by the same name in Greek and Latin, no doubt because the Romans had no equivalent to this god in their own religion and they knew of him only through the Greeks, well before they conquered their territories, probably through trade.

The Roman Apollo therefore had all the attributes of the Greek Apollo and was assigned the same nicknames. He was the god who punished and, in that capacity, carried a bow and arrows.

He was responsible, in particular, for sudden deaths, which were considered the devastating effect of his features. He was the god who brought help and preserved people from harm when they knew how to render him propitious. For that reason, he was the father of Aesculapius, the god of medicine.

He was the god of prophets and exercised this power through numerous oracles, especially the oracle of Delphi, which the Romans went to consult. He was the god of song and of music, he charmed the gods by playing a small harp, and led the chorus of the Muses.

He was the god that protected herds and cattle, which was one of his most important qualifications in the eyes of the Romans.

He was the god who founded cities and laid down their constitutions. He was the god of the sun and of light.

Of all the gods on Olympus, he was the one who had the greatest effect on the human condition. In 212

BC, at the time of the Second Punic War, the Apollonian Games were introduced in Rome. Emperor Augustus was especially devoted to him, and the famous Apollo of the Belvedere represents him with the features of a handsome, vigorous young man.

Diana

Diana was originally a very ancient Italian divinity and she succeeded in retaining her typically Latin features over the ages. She was the goddess of light, as the root of her name indicates – *dies* or day – and this is also suggested by her philological association with Janus, Dianus, god of light, whereby she refers to moonlight.

She had a very ancient temple in Rome, remodelled many times over, on the Mount Aventinus, and her feast day was August the 13th, when purification ceremonies for women took place. Men were usually excluded from these cults, and it was said in Rome that a man who tried to go against this prohibition was torn apart by the goddess's hunting dogs, like Acteon in Greek mythology.

While preserving a number of her original Latin characteristics, the Romans ended up assimilating her to Artemis, Apollo's sister, a friend of the nymphs, a cruel divinity who demanded human sacrifice, and an often pitiless huntress, or, like the Artemis of Ephesus with her multiple breasts, a fertility goddess.

Mercury

Mercury was originally the Latin god of trade and financial gain, ultimately identified with the Hermes of the Greeks. The Romans assigned him all the attributes and fables connected to the latter.

On the other hand, the feast of the *Fetiales* remained faithful to the ancient identity of Mercury who, in the place of the Greek caduceus, carried a sacred branch for his emblem, as a sign of peace.

Mercury was marked by his etymology, which comes from *merx* and *mercator* or merchant. A temple was built for him in the 5th century BC, near the Porta Caprena beside a fountain.

His feast was celebrated in Rome on May the 25th. Merchants, in particular, honored him by visiting the fountain, which was believed to possess magic power.

Mercury was also the official guardian of roads, and played many other roles, including that of messenger and Psychopompos, guiding the souls of the dead.

Vulcan

Vulcan was the god of fire for the Romans. Tatius, the legendary king of the Sabines, was said to have established the cult of Vulcan, as he did for Vesta.

Romulus dedicated a quadriga to Vulcan after his victory over Fidenes, an ancient city in the land of the Sabines, and ordered a temple to be built to his glory alongside that of the divinity of power and glory.

Vulcan was known for his two attributes, the anvil and the hammer, since he was also the patron of blacksmiths. But he was not totally assimilated to Hephaestus, and he retained his own distinct characteristics in strictly Roman mythology. Thus, his emblem in Rome was the sacred lotus, which Romulus planted next to the god's sanctuary.

The temple of Vulcan, like the one dedicated to Vesta, goddess of the hearth, was considered the center of the Roman State, like the Temple of Concord later on. The feast of the *Fornacalia* or *Furnalia,* celebrated on August the 23rd, was dedicated to Vulcan, the protector of ovens.

Vesta

Vesta, the Greek Hestia, goddess of the hearth, is discussed in the section on household gods because she was also destined to private worship, even though she was one of the twelve great divinities of the Roman pantheon.

The Roman State nevertheless associated itself with her in official ceremonies.

Mars

Mars was an ancient Roman god who, although identified with the Greek Ares, should not be confused with him.

In the *Fasti*, Ovid explains that "for a long time, Mars occupied the leading ranks among the divinities of Latium," and he emphasised that "Mars was worshipped in Latium because he presided over war."

The poet demonstrated that all the peoples of Latium had dedicated one of their months to Mars. Indeed, he was the father of Romulus, the founder of Rome, and hence, at that time, the month that bore his name was the first one in the year.

Originally a divinity of the Sabines and the Oscans, he was called Mamers. Mars is simply the contraction of Mavers or Mavors. He is also designated under the name of Maspiter or Marspiter.

Mars was honored in Rome as the god of war. His presence and power over this human activity was such that he was synonymous with war. His priests, known as the Saliens, danced in arms and the field reserved for their military exercises was called the Campus Martius or Field of Mars.

A protector of agriculture like virtually all the Italic divinities, Mars assumed the role of Sylvanus; in his capacity as the god of war, he was given the name of Gradivus, and as the god of civil and administrative relations, he was close to Quirinus and thus a part of the Capitoline Trinity: Jupiter, Mars and Quirinus, the guardian divinities of Rome.

His wife was Neria, the feminine of the Sabine word *nero*, which signified robust. In Rome, the emblems of Mars were less the helmet and arms than the wolf and the woodpecker, which proves he was originally a rustic divinity.

He was, in fact, so closely linked to agriculture that, in the second century before the common era, Cato the Elder advised the owners of farmland in his *Treatise on Agriculture* to purify their lands by praying to Mars with these words:

"Mars, our father, I beg you to look kindly upon me, my household and my people; with this intention I have had a victim led thrice around my fields, my lands and my possessions, so that you might keep them from visible and invisible illnesses, sterility, devastation, calamities and foul weather; that you might foster the growth and abundance of my fruit, my grain, my vines and my trees; that you might preserve the strength of my shepherds and my herds, and grant health and prosperity to me, my household and my people. Thus, to purify my fields, my lands and my possessions, and to perform an expiatory sacrifice, deign to accept these three victims with their udders, which I shall immolate. Mars, our father, accept these three victims for this purpose. Seize the knife to pile up the bread and the cake and offer them. As the pig, the lamb and the calf are immolated, we shall say: be glorified by this victim. [...]"

"If these victims have failed to appease the divinity, we offer this prayer: Mars, our father, if something has displeased you in the sacrifice of three young victims, accept these three instead as expiation. If we presume that one or two of the victims has not been accepted, one shall offer this prayer: Mars, our father, since the sacrifice of the pig was not agreeable to you, accept this one in expiation."

Mars

The god who led the Romans to victory as the head of the armies was represented as a valiant, energetic young man, at the height of his powers. He resembles some of the faces of Greek statues of Alexander the Great.

Following pages
Fragment of a double sacrifice to Mars

On this bas-relief, we can see the priests in charge of sacrificing the victims: a cow, a sheep and a boar. One of the high priests is shown with an axe. At the front of the procession is the Great Pontiff, the leader of Roman religion, his head covered with a hood.
Roman marble from the Field of Mars.

Various temples were dedicated to him in Rome, including one at the Porta Catena on the Appian Way and that of Mars Ultor built under orders from Augustus.

Pluto

Pluto, etymologically "the one who brings wealth", was assimilated to the Greek Hades.

But like all subterranean divinities, those that nourish the earth and help plants to open, Pluto was assimilated to the god Dis Pater, the father of Wealth. Like Hades for Persephone, he was responsible for kidnapping Proserpina.

Venus

Venus, known as the goddess of love well before being identified with the Greek Aphrodite, was not a very important divinity among the Romans, even though poets such as Virgil and Ovid sang her praises and included her in the founding of Rome.

Formerly, she carried the names *Murtea* or *Murcia*, due to her favorite flower, the myrtle, and *Calva* or bald, no doubt because on her feast day, betrothed couples cut off a lock of their hair to offer in sacrifice to Venus. All the great Roman war chiefs sought to place themselves under the protection of this emblematic goddess during the campaigns of the Roman conquest, and they built temples and founded cults dedicated to her.

Caesar, in particular, claimed to have his origins in Aeneas, the son of Mars and Venus. Venus was honored in April, the month that marks the beginning of spring.

In the *Fasti*, Ovid explains: "No season was more appropriate for Venus than the spring, which adorns the earth and opens the bosom of the countryside; the nascent shoots of young wheat push up in the furrows; the bark of vines, overflowing with sap, sees the buds bloom. Such a beautiful season was worthy of Venus. [...]"

"In the spring, she invites the curved vessels to sail across the sea that gave birth to her and no longer fear the threat of winter. Mothers of Latium, and you, young wives, and you who wear neither strips of cloth nor long gowns (Ovid is designating courtesans and prostitutes), come to worship the goddess and give her her due; remove the golden necklaces from the marble statue; remove her rich adornment: she must be entirely washed. When her neck is no longer damp, give her back

her golden necklaces; bring her other flowers, offer her new roses. You yourselves must wash your bodies beneath the green myrtle: Venus orders you to do so and I shall explain why. One day, naked by the shore, she was drying her dripping hair; a group of shameless satyrs came to watch her; the goddess hid herself in the neighboring myrtles and escaped from their gaze.

That is the memory she wishes to preserve through our feasts."

Again in the *Fasti*, the poet sings of the *Vinalia*, or the feasts of Venus in another variation: "young girls with venal loves, it is for you to honor Venus; Venus protects the traffic of those who are destined for every pleasure. For the price of your incense, ask her for beauty and the favor of the people; ask her for caresses that charm and playful words to awaken love. Give your sovereign lady the mint leaves she seeks, along with the myrtle dedicated to her, and garlands woven of reeds entwined with roses."

The Graces

Called the Charites by the Greeks, there were three women in the Roman pantheon who personified grace and beauty in the service of Venus. Some versions of the mythology said that they may have been her daughters.

They embellished the lives of the divinities and human creatures with their charm, their refinement and their delicate manners. They were usually represented as beautiful young girls, either simply nude and holding each other by the hand, or embracing. They sometimes carried musical instruments and were placed under the protection of the rose and the myrtle.

Ceres

Ceres was an Earth goddess who was quickly assimilated to Demeter and worshipped in the land of wheat fields colonised in Campania by the Greeks. Her name was Italic in origin and connected etymologically to *creare* meaning "to create."

Ovid tells the story of her genesis in the *Fasti*: "The first men knew no other harvests than the green grasses with which the earth covered herself without the aid of farming; sometimes they gathered the perennial grasses, sometimes they nourished themselves with the tender foliage crowning the trees; Ceres was the first to invite men to better meals and to abandon acorns for more substantial food; Ceres forced the bull to lower his

Crouching Venus

The canon of beauty revered by the Romans corresponded to a plump young woman with large hips like a mother, who was elegant, supple and graceful in her gestures and movements. It is also the image of Venus, the Roman goddess of love and fertility.

head beneath the yoke and for the first time, the sun warmed the bosom of the newly ploughed earth.

No doubt, she was the most Greek of all the Roman divinities, since the prayers dedicated to her were said in Greek, especially during the festival of the *Cerealia*, held between the 12th and the 19th of April. Everyone dressed in white and offered the goddess cakes of milk and honey and a pig was sacrificed.

At harvest time, a feast was also dedicated to her in August, to which only the women were invited. Ovid writes in the *Fasti* of other cult traditions devoted to Ceres. "O plowmen," he writes, "you may offer to the goddess some wheat, a bit of sparkling salt and a few grains of incense. Light the grass torches. Good Ceres is content with simple gifts, as long as they are offered by pure hands." Then Ovid relates the episode about the kidnapping of Ceres' daughter, Proserpina, the Persephone of Greek mythology, which is essential to understand the symbolism of the goddess. One day, Ceres went to a feast accompanied by Proserpina who went off to walk in the surrounding countryside with a few companions, gathering flowers and plants, especially lilies and saffron.

Her uncle, Pluto, the Greek Hades, king of the Underworld, spied her and immediately carried her off on his steeds to his underground kingdom. Warned by the terrified cries of Proserpina's companions, Ceres set out in search of her daughter, wandering across the earth and even through the heavens. Jupiter finally told her that Pluto had wedded Proserpina and, before the weeping of Ceres, agreed to allow the queen of the Underworld to spend six months of the year in the heavens.

"Thus," concludes Ovid, "Ceres' face and soul recovered their serenity; she laid a garland of wheatears upon her hair; the fields, which had grown barren while Ceres was wandering, were again covered with abundant harvests and the wheat lofts could barely hold these treasures." This mythological parable recounts the cycle of the seasons, and explains the death and rebirth of Nature.

Neptune

Originally, Neptune, the main god of seas and waters among the Romans, was undoubtedly a small Italic divinity that ensured the dampness required for abundant cultivation, for the Romans were never sailors. His temple was found on the Field of Mars and, on his festival day, tents were put up with branches and the people feasted beneath them. The Roman poets, who found little inspiration in Neptune, assimilated him entirely to Poseidon.

Saturn

Saturn was originally a fabled king of Italy that the Romans ended up identifying with the Greek god Cronos, father of the gods of Olympus, and consequently of Jupiter, Neptune, Pluto, etc. But, in reality, there was no resemblance between the attributes of the two divinities, except that both were considered the earliest gods in their respective countries. On the other hand, there was a resemblance between Demeter (Ceres) and Saturn.

Indeed, whatever the Greeks had attributed to Demeter, the Italians and later the Romans attributed to Saturn. The name of Saturn was derived from *sero, sevi, satum* meaning "to sow", and he was considered the founder of the civilisation and social order so closely linked to agriculture.

For the same reason, his reign was regarded as the golden age of Italy. As agriculture is the source of all wealth, his wife was Ops, the symbol of abundance. Tradition held that the god came to Italy during the reign of Janus, and Macrobius echoes the story in the *Saturnalia*, where he was given hospitality.

At the foot of a hill known as the Saturnian, on the road leading to the Capitoline Hill, a temple was built later on and dedicated to Saturn. During his stay, Saturn was said to have taught agriculture to the Roman people, bringing them from a savage state into civilised, moral life. As a result, the whole country was given the name Saturnia Telius, the land of Saturn or of abundance.

According to a later tradition, the name Latium was said to be derived from the verb *lateo* meaning "to be hidden", due to the disappearance of Saturn, who was suddenly ravished from the earth and for that reason, considered a divinity of the lower world.

The festival of the *Saturnalia* was one of the most famous in Roman religion. According to Roman tradition, the statue of Saturn was hollowed out and filled with oil, the symbol of fertility in Latium where olive trees grew.

He was represented holding a billhook in one hand with woolen strips around his feet. The temple of Saturn was used as the public treasury, since he had taught King Janus to strike money and several tables of laws were placed there.

Triumph of Neptune and Amphitrite

With his wife Amphitrite, Neptune dominates the waters filled with fish and sea animals. Indeed, he protects navigation, but especially fishermen. He crosses the seas in a chariot drawn by steeds, with a trident as the scepter of his sovereignty over all the oceans.
3rd century Roman mosaic.

The Roman exception: the triad of Jupiter, Mars and Janus

The Romans were the only people in the ancient Mediterranean Basin to venerate Triads, guardian, political divinities that played a crucial role in the combined operations of State and Religion.

The number three, a magic number, the number of the Trinity, was not unknown to these cults.

The first of the Triads included Jupiter, Mars and Janus. With their dominant attributions, these three gods were, by their very nature, the protectors of the Roman nation, the first as the god of the heavens, the second as the god of war and the third as the god of conception of life and the birth of the world.

This triad was somewhat modified when Janus was replaced by Quirinus, under legendary circumstances reported by Ovid in the *Fasti*. Indeed, Romulus was worshipped under that name, "either because, as a warrior god in Olympus, he wished to be given the name of the javelin which the ancient Sabines called a *curis*, or because as the king of the Quirites (patrician senators of Rome), he adopted the name, or finally, because he united the city of Cures to the territory of Rome."

"After his death, he appeared to the Roman senator Julius Proculus saying: 'Let the Quirites cease weeping for me: I rank among the gods and these tears offend me; offer incense instead, and let a pious gathering worship me under the name of Quirinus. […]' Proculus assembled the people and announced Romulus' commands to them. A temple was raised in honor of the new god; a hill received his name, and every year the feast of the father of the Romans returns on the same day."

The cult of this Triad was handed down to the main Flamines or the public priests of the Roman people, who were three in number.

Another triad came into being in the royal Rome of the Etruscans that included Jupiter, Juno and Minerva. Worshipped on the Capitoline Hill, they came to be known as the Capitoline Triad. This triad consisted of protective guardians who were the core of the political and religious system of the Roman State, a role they played until the end.

Garni Temple in Armenia

The ancient temple in Garni, with its harmonious, human-sized proportions, is quite similar to the "Square Houses" in Nîmes and Vienne, France, like so many others in the Roman empire dedicated to Augustus, who restored Roman religion.

ROMAN HEROES

The Greeks were known for their cult of heroes, great men and legendary demigods together with their history and epic tales. The Romans were not inclined to hero worship, those poetic, sentimental cults rooted in ancient literature and mythology, but those in power soon realised the benefits that could be obtained from such cults, especially during the reign of Augustus.

When Roman institutions changed and the Republic gave way to the Empire, poets such as Virgil and Ovid, and many others as well, exalted Roman national heroes so that the State might take advantage of divine, epic and heroic origins in order better to impose itself.

Hercules

The most famous demigod in the mythology is Hercules. Of course, the Romans did not invent him. They copied his famous twelve labors from those of the Greek Heracles, but they also succeeded in exalting the character to such an extent that one of the Emperors of the Tretrachy, founded by Diocletian, was to be considered an avatar of Hercules and placed under his protection. Roman art represented him many times over, and the most beautiful image of the hero that has come down to us is that of Hercules Farnesi. The hero is in repose, leaning on his right arm, with his head resting on his left hand.

According to the Roman writers, the cult of Hercules in Rome was connected to the hero's expedition to find the magnificent cattle of the king of Spain, Geryon, a three-headed or three-bodied monster, beyond the Straits of Gibraltar called, for that reason, the Pillars of Hercules.

They claimed that Hercules visited Italy upon his return, and abolished human sacrifice among the Sabines, established fire worship, and killed the monstrous Cakus who had stolen his magnificent cattle.

Thus, the Latins, especially their celebrated King Evander, worshipped Hercules as a god. In exchange, Hercules taught them how his cult was to be established and entrusted it to two aristocratic families from Rome, the Potitii and the Pinarii.

In Rome, the cult of Hercules was connected to the Muses, and he was represented with a lyre, which is contrary to Greek practice in which the Muses were associated with Apollo. The process whereby Hercules became a hero is recounted by Ovid in *The Metamorphoses*. The son of Jupiter and Alcmena, the spouse of Amphitryon, who was suffering atrociously after donning the famous poison tunic of Nessus, went up to the top of Mount Etna, had a pile of wood erected, placed himself upon it and ordered it to be set on fire.

"Already the victorious flame was crackling," wrote Ovid, "and spreading all around the pyre; it attacked the limbs of the hero who remained calm and seemed to scorn its reach. The gods of Olympus were distressed at the suicide of Hercules and opened their hearts to his father, Jupiter. The latter replied: 'Your alarm gives me joy, inhabitants of Olympus, and I rejoice from the bottom of my heart to be called the master and father of a grateful people and to see that my son has found new support in your solicitude. Although he owes this interest to no one but himself and his miraculous labors, I myself am grateful to you."

"But close your faithful souls to vain alarms, and scorn the pyre that burns on Eta: the one who has vanquished everything will be able to vanquish the fires that you see: they will make their power felt in that part of himself he received from his mother (the mortal Alcmena); but what he has received from me is eternal, imperishable, safe from death and flames. When this other part of his being has left the earth, I will receive it in the celestial home and I proudly maintain that all the gods will be satisfied…"

Head of Hercules

Here, Hercules has just completed the first of his twelve labors, by strangling the Nemean lion, and covering his own head with the pelt.
Replica of a 5t[h] century BC original. Classical Greece.

Following pages
Hercules and Geryon

We recognise Hercules wearing the skin of the Nemean lion, and Geryon, who occupied a special place in specifically Roman mythology, with his three heads and three shields.

"The gods applauded this speech… However, the flame had consumed everything it could destroy; there was nothing left of Hercules that was recognizable, nothing of what he had received from his mother: he retained only the features in which Jupiter had engraved his image. As we see a snake rejuvenate, when it has shed age along with its skin and spread the bright colors of its new scales, thus the Hero of Tirynth, released from his mortal shell, lived on in the best part of himself; one would say that he had become greater and had taken on divine majesty. The sovereign master of the gods lifted him from the flanks of a cloud on a chariot pulled by four steeds and put him among the stars dazzling with light." That is what the Romans called an apotheosis and all of their heroes, born like Hercules, from the wedding of an immortal with a mortal, as well as many of their emperors, were to be destined for such an apotheosis.

Aeneas

It is therefore not surprising that the legendary founder of Rome, Aeneas, was honored, worshipped and glorified by the Roman State and his praises sung by political figures and historians as well as by the poet Virgil. In the *Aeneid*, which is a veritable biography of a mythical, epic hero, Virgil completes and continues the story told by Homer.

Aeneas, the prince of the Dardanians, a people that lived in the Troad, on the straits of the Hellespont, was the son of Anchises, who was related to Priam, the king of Troy. He was renowned for being strikingly handsome and his beauty was said to equal that of the immortal gods. Anchises was loved by Venus, the goddess of Love, and he gave her a son, Aeneas, whom Homer called Anchisiadus in his *Hymn to Venus*. According to Homer's *Iliad*, Aeneas was born on Mount Ida and he was raised by Alcathous, the husband of his sister Hippodamia.

In his *Hymn to Venus*, however, Homer says that his education was entrusted from birth by his mother to the nymphs of Ida. Anchises fought alongside Priam and his family during the Trojan War. Aeneas did not take part in the conflict, but one day, after being attacked by Achilles near his flocks on Mount Ida, he joined the Trojan army to come to the aid of Priam.

During the struggle, which was to last several years, Aeneas conducted himself like a hero, fearless and irreproachable, to such an extent that the Trojans adored him like a god, on a par with Hector. Like Achilles, the son of a nymph and above all, protected by most of the divinities on the Greek side, Aeneas, on the Trojan side, was the son of Love and the favorite of Apollo. For that reason, several gods protected him during the battles. Like Achilles, Aeneas had a chariot drawn by divine steeds, descendants of those that Jupiter had once given to Love to console her for the kidnapping of Ganymede.

In order to establish the legendary authority of Aeneas, the comparison with Achilles continues. They are mortal enemies. But, within their own camps, they are also hated, Achilles by Agamemnon, Aeneas by Priam, because both kings suspect the heroes of wanting to reign in their stead, the first over Mycenae and no doubt, over all of Greece, and the second over Troy. Aeneas does not hesitate to measure himself against the most courageous warriors, especially Achilles. When he finds himself in danger of perishing at the hands of the fiery hero, Neptune comes to Aeneas' rescue to preserve the divine lineage of the mythical ancestor, Dardanus, son of Zeus and Electra, from whom Anchises and his son descended, as Homer emphazes, "because since at present the race of Priam is odious to the son of Saturn (Neptune is Saturn's son), Aeneas and his posterity down to the last generation will one day reign over the Trojans."

This means that, according to Homer, after the destruction of Troy and the extinction of the race of Priam, Aeneas remained in the Troad and reigned, as did his descendants, over the remaining Trojan people. Indeed, Homer never makes any allusion to a possible emigration of Aeneas nor to a kingdom that he would have founded abroad. The traditions that came after Homer gave other orientations to Aeneas' destiny by suggesting different versions.

The Latin historian, Livy asserts, from the beginning of his *Roman History,* that Aeneas and the Trojan sage Antenor, in view of ancient bonds of hospitality, and because they had constantly spoken in the council of Troy in favor of peace and of returning Helen, were able to persuade the Greeks to withdraw of their own free will. Other writers claimed that once the city of Troy was taken, Aeneas took refuge among the Dardanians, where he ruled as prince in the citadel, and from there he went to Mount Ida. Pursued by his enemies, he was said to have received an authorization to withdraw freely in exchange for the abandonment of certain mountain strongholds. Still others claimed that Aeneas founded a new kingdom in Epirus or in Thessaly.

The tradition of the flight of Aeneas across the seas to Italy is much older than the story told by Virgil in 1 BC. It dates back to the 5th century BC and was reported by the Greek poet Stesichorus. A few centuries later, the story of Aeneas' exodus and his wanderings at sea was told in greater detail. Under the reign of Augustus, Virgil gave us the definitive image of Aeneas pursued, like Ulysses, by the anger of certain divinities, especially Juno and Aeolus, the god of winds and storms. But he was also rescued by Jupiter and Neptune, and above all, by his mother Venus.

Aeneas encouraged his Trojan companions to resist and gave them a speech full of hope: "My companions, he said, it is not today that we are experiencing misfortune; we have already endured much harsher evils. [...] Summon your courage, banish sadness and fear: perhaps one day you shall find these memories sweet. Through so many trials, through so many vicissitudes, we are on our way to Latium where the fates show peaceful dwellings; there we shall be allowed to see the empire of Troy raised again. Harden your hearts to difficulty, and keep yourselves for better days."

Aeneas' arrival in Latium and the foundation of a Trojan colony were variously recounted by Roman historians and poets. According to Virgil's *Aeneid*, confirmed by Ovid's *Metamorphoses*, Aeneas, having lost all hope of saving Troy, left, braving every danger.

As Ovid wrote:" The son of Venus carried off on his shoulders the gods of Troy and his elderly father, (Anchises), a holy and pious burden, the only riches he wished to save." "With his son Ascanius," says Virgil, "his wife Creusa, a daughter of Priam whom he loses during a night of anguish, Aeneas brings together the remaining Trojans on Ida and leaves with them from Antandros, at the foot of the mountain, on twenty vessels."

Among Aeneas' companions is the ship's navigator, Palinurus, who fell into the sea during the crossing and succeeded in swimming to a promontory, which bears his name, where he was killed by the natives. Aeneas was surrounded by his faithful followers who are mentioned in the *Aeneid*, such as Achates, Menestheus, Segestus, Cloanthus who were latinized as Acatius, Memmius, Sergius and Cluentius, and were to be the ancestors of the great Roman families, all proud to descend from the Trojan heroes at the origin of Rome's foundation, who formed the first circle of the aristocracy.

The fleet set sail to Thrace where Aeneas and his companions landed, then it followed the maritime route of Crete, stopping in Delos to pay homage to Apollo, divine master of the island, and protector of Aeneas. Ovid describes the scene in *The Metamorphoses:*

"The king, a priest of Apollo, receives him and leads him to the temple, and then to his home. He shows him the city, the consecrated altars, the two trees to which Latona clung during the pains of childbirth. After pouring incense and wine into the sacrificial flame and burning the entrails of the victims according to the rite, they returned to the palace where, lying on rich rugs, they enjoyed the gifts of Bacchus and Ceres. [...] When the meal was finished, each one yielded to sleep. The Trojans rose with daylight and consulted the oracle of Apollo: "Go and find, it told them, the ancient mother of your race and the shores of your fathers!"

In Crete, the small troop thought they had found the final haven the gods had assigned to them. But a plague was ravaging the island, and all the members of the fleet had to flee. The ships came upon the coast of Sicily where Anchises, the father of Aeneas, died and was buried on Mount Eryx. For seven years, the remaining ships in the Trojan fleet wandered over the seas, until they arrived on the coast of Latium, considered at the time a peaceful shore. But a storm called up by Juno who, because she preferred Carthage, intended to prevent the founding of Rome, drove them back to the African coast near Tunis. Aeneas soon arrived with his companion in Carthage, the city founded by Tyr in Phoenicia.

He was received by Dido, the queen of the city. Dido appeared before him in all her glory, advancing "joyously, among her people, inspiring their work and watching over the future greatness of her empire. Aeneas addressed the queen with these words: "Here he is, that Aeneas that you have been seeking and whom the gods tore from the Libyan waters. O you, who alone had pity on the immense misfortunes of Troy, you who have taken us in, we deplorable remains of the fury of the Greeks, exhausted by the disasters of the land and the sea, and deprived of everything, and who share with us your city and your dwellings, to testify to our proper gratitude, generous Dido, is not in our power. [...] What a happy century is the one that witnessed your birth! What glory for those who gave life to such a great queen. Yes, so long as the rivers flow into the sea; so long as the shadows descend from the mountains and extend over the valleys; so long as the sky shall nourish the stars with its fire, your gifts, your name and your praises shall live in the memory of Aeneas, wherever the fates may call him."

Dido gave Aeneas a sumptuous reception in her palace. "When he arrived at the palace, beautiful Dido took her place beneath a magnificent dais and, leaning against golden pillows, lay there in majestic repose. Aeneas and the Trojans had already gathered; they all lay down on purple beds. Attentive servants poured water on the hands of the guests and dried them with delicate woollen cloth; the gifts of Ceres were drawn from baskets."

Within the palace, fifty women watched over the vast organisation of the feast and burned incense in honor of the Penate gods. A hundred young girls and boys filled the tables with dishes and placed the cups."

At the end of the meal, Aeneas recounted his adventures on land and sea and his dramatic wanderings. Dido, through the will of Juno who influenced Eros, was struck with an overwhelming passion for Aeneas that Jupiter's wife wished to transform into an "incurable malady." The unhappy Dido, writes Virgil in the *Aeneid*, burned with all the fires of love. During a hunting expedition, she withdrew into a cave with Aeneas: "That day was the beginning of death for Dido, and her first day of misfortune. Now nothing could touch her, neither decency nor honor, it was no longer a secret love she pretended to hide; she called it a marriage, using that name as a cover for her deplorable weakness."

The gods were worried about this love and they sent Mercury to remonstrate with Aeneas and force him to leave Dido and her empire. Aeneas attempted to steal away by night from the shores of Africa as silently as possible with his ships and his companions.

But Dido got wind of his flight and ran to Aeneas to tell him of her despair: "Cruel one!" she said, "it is under a winter sky that your fleet casts off and despite the stormy waters, you make haste to sail the high seas! For you I have made myself odious to the nations of Libya, to the nomad kings and even to my Tyrians; for you I have lost my modesty; I have lost the sole good that made me equal to the gods, my renown. [...] Had you left me, before taking flight, some sweet proof of your love, if I had a child that I might see grow up in my court who would merely remind me of his father's features, I would not be so utterly captive and abandoned."

Aeneas was torn by this love, since the gods had enjoined him to go to the coast of Italy, "his new country", he said. Then Dido cursed him and once Aeneas' fleet had gone, she stabbed herself upon a pyre, which she had lit to consume her. The Trojans, led by

Aeneas, made a stop in Sicily, where they received the hospitality of King Acestes, a descendant of the Trojan Egesta or Segesta whose father had sent her away to Sicily so she would not be sacrificed to the sea monster sent by Neptune, and who married the river god Crinisius. After celebrating the funeral games near his father's tomb on Mount Eryx, Aeneas left the great island. The Trojan hero, surrounded by his gods and the Palladium, the image of the goddess Minerva on whom the salvation of the entire city depended, arrived in Latium and laid the foundations for the Roman nation.

The Romans rallied to this last version, which enabled Julius Caesar , from the Julia family, to claim to be a descendant of Iulius or Ascanius, the son of Aeneas, but above all, naturally, to have the goddess Venus as his ancestor. Aeneas entered sometime later into the port of Cumae, founded by the Greeks in Campania. There he met the Sibyl who invited him to descend into Hades for a visit, in these words: "Keep your distance, the profane," she cried, "keep your distance and all of you leave the sacred wood! And you, Aeneas, walk with me, your sword out of its sheath: this is the moment, Aeneas, to have courage and an intrepid heart." Aeneas then descended into the Underground and Virgil describes in detail this frightening, subterranean world where his hero advances, meeting dead companions, war heroes from Troy, enemies and friends and Dido, who comes to join the cursed place.

Aeneas arrives at the Elysian Fields, in the paradise of the just, and above all, led by his father Anchises, he has a vision of the entire history of Rome yet to come, Romulus, the kings, the Tarquins, Caesar and Emperor Augustus.

"Thus Anchises and his son wandered here and there in Elysia and across the airy fields: they went through every region; and Anchises showed Aeneas all these marvels, filling his heart with the burning love of his future greatness" after saying to him: "You, Roman, remember to rule the nations (they will be your arts) and impose peace upon them, spare those who submit and bring down the high and mighty."

Then, leaving Cumae, he went up the Italian peninsula by sea towards the north to reach the port of Caieta. Finally, sailing along the coast, "he discovered from the high sea a vast woods; the Tiber divided it with its delicious waters, and continued swirling and loaded with yellow sands to hurl itself into the sea; around and above the river, thousands of birds, accustomed to its

banks and waves, charmed the air with their song and flew here and there in the woods. There, Aeneas ordered his companions to turn the prow and disembark." This land was Latium, ruled by the king of Laurentum, Latinus, who was growing old and had no son but a daughter, Lavinia. At the sight of a surprising swarm of bees, a soothsayer consulted long ago had said: "I see a foreign warrior arriving on our shores; I see a numerous people coming from the same place as this swarm and dominating from the top of our citadels."

Other wonders alarmed King Latinus who, after many sacrifices, finally heard a voice speak: "Beware, O my son, from giving your daughter to a Latin husband (at the time, Lavinia was being courted by Turnus, the king of the Latins); do not consent to the nuptials being prepared; a stranger shall come, whose blood mixed with yours will raise up to the stars the glory of your name and whose descendants will see everything lit by the sun from one ocean to the other obey their laws and prostrate at their feet."

Latinus understood this message when the arrival of ambassadors dressed in strange garments was announced. He welcomed them with courtesy and granted them his hospitality. Latinus, warned by the voices and miracles, thought about Aeneas, "that foreigner who left a foreign land (who) is indeed the son-in-law announced by the fates and that happy auspices call to succeed his empire; from his union with his daughter must come forth a glorious posterity that will overtake the world through its invincible courage." He welcomed Aeneas with friendship and even gave him land upon which his guest could found a city. Moreover, he promised him the hand of his daughter, Lavinia.

But Amata, the wife of Latinus, spurred on by Juno who sought the end of Aeneas and the offspring of the Trojans, rebelled against these plans and incited Turnus, the young, valiant king of the Rutulians, to whom Lavinia was promised, to take up arms against Aeneas. Latinus realised that Juno and some of the gods were still hostile towards him, but he maintained his choice. Taking "as witnesses the gods and the air he breathes", in the face of the threat of a conflict between Aeneas and Turnus and the fury of the gods, he cried out: "Alas, we are crushed by the fates, carried off by the tempest. […] And you, Turnus, a sad torture awaits you and you shall implore, but too late, the inflexible gods. For me, I am assured of rest and I am arriving at my end: I shall lose nothing but a quiet death."

"Thus he spoke, closed himself into his palace and abandoned the reins of his empire." Mezentius, the king of Caere, as well as other Italian warriors such as Aventinus and his ferocious fighters, joined the army of Turnus. Latinus, out of weakness and weariness, did not oppose the vast coalition that was forming against Aeneas, and did not even keep his promise to give him his daughter Lavinia in marriage. Aeneas was visited in a dream by the river Tiber who encouraged him to fight with flattering words: "Son of the gods, you who carry upon our shores Ilion torn from enemy hands and who preserves for us the eternal Pergamum; hero so long awaited in the fields of Latium, here is your assured dwelling, here must you settle your Penates. […] Here is the place where you shall build your city; there awaits the end of your labors; and barely thirty years will have gone by before your son Ascanius founds Alba, the city with the celebrated name.

Aeneas allied himself with Evander, son of Mercury and the nymph Carmenta who, after arriving from Acadia, had colonised the Palatine and had the city of Pallantium built at the mouth of the Tiber and had thus, in a sense, preceded him in the conquest of Latium. Violent fighting opposed the armies of Turnus and Aeneas, who was helped by his mother, Venus, and by the god, Mars. For that war was the subject of often ferocious consultations among the gods on Olympus, some of whom favored Turnus, and the others, Aeneas.

Latinus realised his error and called Turnus and said to him: "I was forbidden to unite my daughter in marriage with any of the suitors of ancient Italy; the oracles of the gods and their interpreters ceaselessly told me the order of the fates. Vanquished by the friendship that bound me to you, vanquished by blood ties and the tears of a desolate wife, I broke all of my sacred commitments. I took from Aeneas the daughter I had promised him; I raised up impious arms against him. Since that fatal day, you see, Turnus, such misfortune, such bloody disasters have befallen me."

Then, King Latinus proposed a peaceful arrangement to Turnus: "If you, Turnus, are dead, I must bind these new allies to my fortune, why then would I not instead cease the fighting and preserve your life? What will the Rutulians, my own blood, say, what will all of Italy say, if I deliver you over to death, if you perish for having asked for the hand of my daughter and the title of son-in-law?" Turnus refused to listen to his appeals to reason and the fighting resumed.

Mercury orders Aeneas to abandon Dido

In ancient mythologies, heroes were not always free, but rather subject to gods who interfered in their lives. Thus Mercury, acting on orders from Jupiter despite the hostility of his wife Juno, orders Aeneas to leave Carthage and Dido. The latter, who is in love with Aeneas, could not bear to go on living after his departure.
Orazio Samacchini, 1532-1577.

The Trojans settle in Libya

Arriving by sea, the Trojans who survived the Trojan War land with their ships on the coast of Libya. They are depicted as industrious and active, a fitting portrayal of a people who would open trading posts all around the Mediterranean.
Limoges enamel by the Master of the Aeneid, circa 1530.

Turnus, drunk with fury, "carried the eager flame to the Trojan fleet," Ovid recounts in *The Metamorphoses*, "and fire threatened what had escaped the waves."

"Already it was devouring pitch, wax and every material that could feed its flames; already it ran along the masts, and set the sails afire, the rowing benches began to smoke. But the venerated mother of the gods, Cybele, remembered that Aeneas' vessels were made of pine from Mount Ida." She cried, "I shall not allow the fire to consume the sons of my forest," and she transformed the ships: "The timber softened into the shape of a human body: the rounded sterns became heads and faces, the yards new arms, the oars hands and feet that cleaved the waters, the ships' flanks yielded, hulls turned into trunks and ropes into wavy hair: they were the new Naiads." But Turnus refused to abdicate and went back to fighting.

Ovid imagined the scene in the *Fasti*: "Two kings went forward with great pomp. Latinus was borne on a chariot pulled by four steeds; a crown of twelve rays, like the sun, shone around his temples. [...] Turnus appeared, pulled by two white steeds, brandishing two javelins with large points. Aeneas, father of the Romans, went towards the same point. He was immediately recognisable by the fires shooting from his celestial shield and the flashing of his divine weapons. Ascanius was at his side."

After making sacrifices to the gods, signs appeared in the heavens. The fighting resumed between Aeneas' Trojans and Turnus' troops. Aeneas was wounded by an arrow, but with the help of his mother, the wound was healed. Turnus and the Rutulians seemed about to win. There were many dead and wounded and the outcome of the fighting still uncertain. Then Turnus rushed into the battle with his chariot and cried: "Stop, Rutulians, and you, Latins, hold back your arrows."

'Whatever the fate of this fight, it shall be mine. It is only just that I alone should bear the pain for violating the treaty, that I alone should fight.' At these words, everyone drew back and left a wide space between the two armies. Meanwhile, Aeneas, at the very sound of Turnus' name, left the walls and high towers of Laurentum […] thundered his frightening armor […] Trojans, Rutulians, Italians, everyone's gaze was fixed upon the two rivals […] Latinus himself was astonished at the sight of these two great warriors, born so far away from each other, who were now about to fight in single combat and mix their blows. Hardly had the field opened when both combatants dashed out, hurled their javelins from a distance, leapt at each other and attacked, crashing shield against shield, bronze against bronze. […]"

Turnus leapt, straightened with all the force of his body, raised his arm and sword and struck a blow against Aeneas that he thought sure. But the Rutulian's treacherous sword shattered. "Turnus fled, pursued by Aeneas. Aeneas tried to pull a javelin he had thrown into an olive tree and succeeded through the invisible intervention of his mother Venus." Again Juno wished to favor Turnus, but Jupiter forbade her to intervene. Aeneas launched his javelin; when it landed in Turnus' thigh, he begged for mercy. Aeneas appeared to be giving in, when he spied around Turnus' shoulders the skin of a child, Pallas, the son of Evander, one of the Trojan's allies.

This time his wrath was terrible: "And so, still adorned with the skins of our people, you would escape me! At these words, Aeneas plunged his boiling sword into Turnus' chest: the chill of death flowed through his limbs, he moaned and his angry soul fled to the Manes." The *Aeneid* ends with this episode. But in addition to Virgil's epic poem, we have other versions of Aeneas' tale, particularly by Ovid in *The Metamorphoses* and Livy in his *Roman History*.

Aeneas married Lavinia and gave the name of his wife to the city of Lavinium he founded. Lavinia gave birth to Ascanius. Turnus, furious at having been dispossessed of his fiancée, took up arms against Aeneas and Latinus by allying himself with the Rutulians, the inhabitants of a narrow strip of land along the coast of Latium, south of the Tiber, with a principal city named Ardea. In the first fight, the Rutulians were vanquished and Latinus was killed. To achieve victory, Turnus united with Mezentius, king of Caere and Agylla of Etruria. In the face of this coalition, Aeneas took action, and in order to reconcile himself with the indigenous people governed by King Latinus, he decided to ally them with the Trojans and chose the name 'Latins' as their common denominator. He led them to victory over Mezentius and his son Lausus who were killed, along with Turnus.

Thus ended Aeneas' work on earth. According to other traditions, he was said to have disappeared into sudden shadows, accompanied by claps of thunder and lightning, during the battle against the Etruscans on the banks of the Numicius. According to *The Metamorphoses*, this is how it happened: "[…] Aeneas had only to take his place in the heavens. Venus had won the suffrage of the gods in his favor. She put her caressing arms around Jupiter's neck: 'O my father', she said, 'you have never been strict and harsh with your daughter. Be even more indulgent today, I beg of you. Give my son, Aeneas, who recognises you as his forbear, a place among the gods, be it the lowliest […]'. All Olympus applauded at her words and Juno ceased to wear a cold, unmoving look: she consented with a smile. Jupiter replied to Venus: 'You are both worthy of this favor, you who request it, and the one for whom it is asked: receive it, my daughter, I granted it to you'. "Venus, overjoyed, gave thanks to him; she mounted her chariot, borne by doves, and flew through the air and alighted on the banks of the Numicius. […] She ordered the river to wash away the mortal parts subject to decay and make them vanish in its silent waters. The river obeyed. The flowing waters carried off the perishable part of the hero. The divine essence alone remained. The goddess covered his purified body with a celestial odor and breathed upon his lips a mixture of nectar and ambrosia. Aeneas became a god."

His faithful followers, those who had accompanied his epic adventures and his political destiny which enabled him to gather the main towns of Latium together into the leaven from which the future great Rome would rise, erected a sanctuary in his name on the banks of the Numicius with this inscription carved on its pediment: *Patris dei Indigetis*: "To the indigenous god of the Fatherland." Later, Aeneas would be honored under the prestigious name of Jupiter Indiges, the Jupiter of the country, whereas Latinus, Aeneas's father-in-law, was ranked among the gods under the name of Jupiter Latiaris.

Thirty years after the mysterious, holy vanishing of Aeneas, his son, Ascanius, under the name of Iule, founded Alba Longa, and was the first of the long line of kings of that city, as he was considered by Caesar, of the family of Iule or Julius, as his ancestor.

Romulus, Remus and the She-Wolf

This moving, realistic sculpture shows Romulus and Remus, the founders of Rome, suckling the famous She-Wolf, whose head is inclined towards the twins in a familiar attitude among animals, clearly conveying the attention they give to their young. Decorative element of a Roman chariot, Roman bronze, Lebanon.

Romulus

Aeneas, the mythical father of Rome as it came into being during the *Aeneid*, an epic poem linked to Homer's *Iliad,* is not the only Roman hero, even though he is among the most famous. The twins Romulus and Remus, who were the first sovereigns of Rome, and as it were, the founders of the celebrated city, also remain among the heroes of the City among cities. Their story was familiar to all Romans and the She-Wolf feeding them with her milk remains one of the great sculptures of Roman civilisation.

According to the tradition, echoed by Latin historians and poets, Romulus and Remus were the sons of Rhea Silvia and of Mars, the god of war. Silvia was indeed the daughter of Numitor, himself a descendant of Iule, the son of Aeneas. Thus the Romans cleverly linked their mythical father to the founders of their city. Numitor had been dispossessed by his brother Amulius of the throne of Alba Longa, a city located between

Mount Alban and the lake of the same name, near the present convent of Palazzola.

Rhea Silvia, a vestal dedicated to perpetual virginity, had succumbed to the seduction of Mars and found herself pregnant with twins. After the birth of the two children, Silvia was drowned in the Tiber for failing to honor her vow of chastity. "Her father's brother," writes Ovid in the *Fasti*, "was on the throne at the time; he ordered the children to be taken and drowned in the Tiber. Fool! Did you not know that one of them had to be Romulus? The king's ministers regretfully went to carry out his cruel orders; they wept as they brought the twins to the designated spot. Winter rains had swollen the Albula, which took the name of the Tiber after Tiberius perished in its waters. Boats sailed on the place where our forums stand today, and the deep walls of our Circus. When they arrived at the place, they were forced to stop, and one of them cried out: 'How these children resemble each other and how beautiful they both are! Yet this one looks more vigorous than the other. If birth can be read

upon the face, if their features do not lie, I seem to see signs of celestial origin. Yet if some god had been the author of your days, he would come to your rescue in this critical moment; your mother would protect you if she hadn't needed protection herself, unfortunate creature! Brothers in life, be brothers also in death and let the river submerge you together'.

"Thus he spoke, and released his burden; just as everyone was going away, their cheeks bathed in tears, the children, as if guessing their peril, let out a plaintive wail in unison. The basket that carried them, a fragile skiff for such great destinies as were entrusted to it, floated on the surface of the waves at first; then it landed at the foot of a thick copse, where it was held in the sludge deposited by the river as it flows away. There rose a tree that had not disappeared altogether; and what we now call the Ruminal fig tree was the fig tree of Romulus. Who would believe that the abandoned twins were brought by a stroke of good fortune to a she-wolf that had just become a mother? The ferocious beast did

not hurt the children; on the contrary, they would owe their life to her; and they who were condemned to die, were fed the milk of a she-wolf. She stopped, caressed these tender newborns with her tail, and licked them all over their small bodies. They were indeed the sons of Mars; they did not tremble, but seized the teats of the she-wolf and drank their full of a nourishing milk that was not intended for them."

Let us listen to Livy tell the rest in the beginning of his *Roman History*: "The intendant of the king's flocks found her licking the infants. Faustulus (it is said this was the man's name) carried them home and put them under the care of his wife Larentia", who would be divinised by the Romans under the name of Acca Larentia. "Thus the children were born and raised. They had barely reached adolescence when, disdaining the idleness of the sedentary life and watching over flocks, hunting took them into the surrounding forests. But, drawing strength and courage from their fatigue, they no longer stopped at giving chase to ferocious beasts, they attacked brigands loaded with loot and shared their skins among the shepherds. A crowd of young shepherds, growing more numerous every day, took part in their dangers and their games. At that time, the feast of *Lupercales* was celebrated on Mount Palatine […]." Romulus and Remus joined in. "In the middle of the festivities, which had been announced earlier, and surprised by the brigands furious at seeing their loot carried off by the twins, Romulus defended himself with vigor, but Remus was captured. The brigands delivered their prisoner to King Amulius, accusing him of every evil that had befallen them. Remus was then handed over to the deposed King Numitor. From the beginning, Faustulus held out the hope that these infants were of royal blood, for he knew about the king's order to expose newborn children and he had taken them in at that moment. By chance, Numitor, who was the master of Remus, learned that the brothers were twins, and given their age and their noble pride, the memory of his grandsons was rekindled in his heart."

Numitor was ready to learn the truth and to confound Amulius. When the latter realized this, he fomented a plot against him. "Romulus, too weak to act openly, was careful not to come leading his shepherds. He ordered them to come to the palace at an appointed hour by different paths. There they fell upon the king: at the head of Numitor's men, Remus gave them a hand and Amulius was massacred. Numitor was put back on the throne of Alba, Romulus and Remus conceived the idea of founding a city on the site as testimony to the dangers they had experienced in their childhood. […]. Mixed in with these projects was the thirst for power, an illness they had inherited."

They argued over the place where the future city was to be raised. "They were twins, and the prerogative of age could not be a decisive factor between them. They left it to the guardian divinities of the place to designate, through oracles, which one should give his name and laws to the new city, and then withdrew, Romulus to Mount Palatine and Remus to Mount Aventine, to mark out the walls of the oracle."

Ovid recounts the rest of this veritable epic adventure in the *Fasti*:

"Remus saw six birds, and his brother saw twelve in succession; the pact was executed and the city was raised according to Romulus' wishes. An auspicious day was chosen to mark out with a plow the contour of the walls. The feast of Pales arrived, and she was to give the signal for the work to begin. First a deep pit was dug; grain and fruit and earth from the surrounding fields were thrown in. As soon as the pit was filled, an altar was raised; the fire was lit and the wood burst in the new hearth. Then Romulus, seizing the handle of the plow, marked out the rampart walls with the plowshare; a white cow was attached to the yoke along with an ox as white as she.

King Romulus pronounced these words: "Jupiter and you, Mars, my father, and you, venerable Vesta, assist me in this moment as I found Rome. I also invoke you all, gods whose presence my piety requires that I implore, that my work be raised under your auspices! May this city last for many years, may it command the universe, may it dictate its laws to the East and the West!" "Thus he prayed, and on his left, he heard the thunder of Jupiter, a favorable sign; on his left, lightning crisscrossed the sky. The citizens, who were transported with joy at this good omen, immediately laid the foundations and in a few days, had built the city walls. Celer, the god of swiftness, hastened the works at the request of Romulus himself: 'Watch over this spot,' he said, 'see to it that no one climbs over these walls and the furrow marked out by the plow. He who so dares shall be punished by death.'

"Remus ignored this prohibition, and laughed at the weakness of the ramparts: 'Do you believe that people will be safe behind these walls?', he asked and at the moment, jumped over them. Immediately, Celer punished the stroke of bravura with a blow of his hoe, Remus fell to the ground, bathed in his own blood. At the news, Romulus contained the tears that were brimming in his eyes. He stifled the pain in his breast. He must not be seen weeping. In this, he imitated the boldest hearts. 'Thus shall perish,' he cried, 'any enemy that comes over these ramparts!' However, he gave his brother funeral honors, and then no longer held back his tears. Too long contained, his pious regret burst forth. He gave the last kisses to the coffin: 'Farewell', he cried, 'farewell, brother whose death I did not wish'. He perfumed the body that the funeral pyre would consume. […]. Those who would later be called Quirites (senators) offered their tears for young Remus and sprinkled the fatal pyre. Soon the flames had consumed everything."

It should be noted that, in his *Roman History*, Livy presented a more tragic, less toned-down version of the death of Remus than Ovid's account. In the historian's version, Romulus is responsible for the death of his brother. It is interesting to compare the two narratives, and observe what a poet wishing to flatter the imperial power and what an historian had to say about the same legendary event:

"A quarrel (between the two brothers) broke out, which in their anger degenerated into a bloody fight. Struck in the fray, Remus fell dead. According to the most widely held tradition, out of derision, Remus had leaped over the new ramparts raised by his brother in a single bound and Romulus, carried away in his rage, killed him, crying out 'Thus shall perish whoever would cross over our walls."

Livy continues: "Romulus was now the sole master, and the new city took the name of its founder. Mount Palatine on which it had been raised was the first place he took care to fortify. […]. Once the religious ceremonies were regularly established, he brought together a general assembly of the people that alone could give force to the laws if they were to form a nation, and dictated his own; persuaded that the surest way to make them sacred in the eyes of such coarse men was to aggrandize himself with outward signs of command, among other distinctive marks of his dignity, he decided to surround himself with twelve lictors. That number is thought to have been based on the twelve vultures that had foretold the empire. […]."

"However, the city grew and its walls were expanded each day, measured more by hopes for the future population than the needs of the current one. To give some reality to this grandeur, Romulus, faithful to the ancient policy of city founders that said the land had engendered inhabitants, opened a refuge in the place closed today by a fence at the bottom of the Capitol, between two woods where murderers and fugitive slaves could find asylum," writes Ovid, this time, in the *Fasti*, "and could no longer be troubled by their victims, by the law or by their masters. The good news made the rounds of the region and soon the city was full of a great number of highly disreputable people."

"Romulus," writes Livy, "satisfied with the forces he had conquered, subjected them to regular direction. He instituted a hundred senators, either because this number seemed sufficient to him, or because he could not find more who were worthy of the honor. What is certain is that they were called Fathers, and that name became their title of honor; their descendants were called Patricians. But Romulus observed that women were lacking in this new population."

"Shrewdly", writes Ovid in the *Fasti*, Romulus thus came up with a stratagem, which soon turned, into a trap. He announced that games would be celebrated in Rome in honor of the god Consus, the god of secret deliberations, whose altar he had found buried in the ground. These festivities were to be called the Consualia. He invited his closest neighbors, the Latins and Sabines, to the merrymaking. Taking advantage of the help of the people and the crowd taking part in the ceremonies, the young men of Rome, duly instructed by Romulus, rushed upon the foreigners, knocking many unconscious and amid the resulting of the confusion, carried off the young girls by force and disappeared with them."

The violence of these kidnappings immediately led to war between the Romans and the Sabine and Latin peoples. The fighting was long and fierce, and it seemed the conflict would never end. At this point, we shall borrow from Livy's far more spectacular, picturesque and detailed narrative: "Then the same Sabine women, whose kidnapping had set off the war, in their despair overcame the timidity natural to their sex; they threw themselves intrepidly, their hair flying and their clothes in disorder, between the two armies and the hail of arrows: they stopped the hostilities, contained the fury, and addressing first their fathers, then their husbands, they called upon them not to soil with the sacred blood of a father-in-law or a son-in-law nor imprint with the stigmata of parricide the brows of children they had already conceived, or the sons and grandsons of those children: 'If this kinship, in which we are the bonds, if our marriages are odious in your eyes, turn your wrath upon us; we, the source of this war, we the cause of the wounds and massacre of our spouses and their fathers, we would prefer to perish than to live without you, as widows or orphans'. All the men, leaders and soldiers, were moved. The prayers of the Sabine women were heard. Not only, Ovid tells us, did "the two peoples make peace, but they proclaimed that their nations would henceforth become one and the same."

"However this union did not last. Titus Tatius, king of the Sabines, who shared the throne with Romulus, was approached during a feast in Lanuvium by a few Laurentians from the city of Laurentum in Latium, who claimed to be have been outraged by his relatives. In vain Tatius refused to be humiliated, and was immediately killed. Romulus, who had no doubt guided the revolt and the murder, henceforth reigned alone over the Romans and the Sabines."

The reign of Romulus lasted thirty-seven years until the day his father, the god Mars, according to Ovid in *The Metamorphoses*, spoke thus to the sovereign of the gods and men: "It is time, O my father, now that Roman power stands on a solid foundation. […]. It is time to keep your promises to me and to my son, to carry Romulus up from the earth and bring him to the heavens. Formerly, in the presence of all the gods, you told me: 'One of your sons shall be immortal: you shall be able to raise him to Olympus'. You said this. Let your word be accomplished! Jupiter made a sign, the heavens were covered with dark clouds and lightning made Rome tremble. At this sign, which enabled him to carry away Romulus, Mars , his lance in hand, mounted proudly on his bloodied chariot, spurred on his steeds, crossed for a moment the plains of the air and descended to the top of Mount Palatine, crowned with forests. Just as Romulus was rendering justice to his people, he was carried away. The mortal remains of the hero dissolved in the air, like a lead bullet vigorously launched by the spirit of revolt. He assumed a divine shape, more worthy of celestial banquets, the form of Quirinus dressed in a purple toga."

Livy adds the following to Ovid's account: "All of them, by unanimous acclamation, saluted Romulus, God, son of God, king and god of the Roman city. They asked him, they begged him to look always favorably upon his posterity." Shortly after this wonder occurred, Julius Proculus, a senator with high authority, went forward to the middle of the Senate and spoke: 'Romans, the father of this city, Romulus, who suddenly descended from the heavens, appeared to me this morning at daybreak. Struck with terror and respect, I stood unmoving, trying to obtain from him through my prayers to be allowed to contemplate his face: "Go", he said, "announce to your fellow citizens that this city I have founded, my Rome, shall be queen of the world; such is the will of heaven. That the Romans shall give themselves over wholly to the science of war; that they shall know, and their descendants after them, that no human power can resist the weapons of Rome." 'At these words', continued Proculus, 'he rose into the air'."

According to pure tradition, that was how the apotheosis of Romulus took place. There are other, less glorious accounts according to which senators, unhappy at being governed by a tyrant, killed him in the midst of the shadows and the storm, cut his body into pieces and carried off beneath their robes the bloody debris of their king.

It has often been said that Rome and its gods and heroes were nothing but a pale or awkward copy of Athens and its mythology, a view that reveals the same contempt once shown towards certain Western products copied by Japanese civilization. For a long time, it was fashionable to consider Rome condescendingly, as the illegitimate child of its Hellenic and oriental conquests. This conception of history, which claims that the ancient Greeks alone were masters and the Romans devoid of any originality or creativity is fortunately beginning to disappear, thanks to the work of Latin scholars and historians, from Jérôme Carcopino to Pierre Grimal and Claude Nicolet.

Rome was already in existence and ruled by kings, particularly the famous Tarquinian dynasty, when Athens reached its peak in the 5th century, known as the century of Pericles and of the invention of oligarchic democracy. The two cities did not maintain ongoing relations, unless perhaps through the Etruscan empire and its trading posts. Both had already invented their gods, their cults and their heroes, before they were brought into comparison with the conquest of Athens by Rome.

Their civilizations were different: the first relied on sailors, the second on infantrymen, one was born of the sea, and the other of the land. Their early gods were also different, with the Athenian pantheon enriched by cosmopolitan and oriental contributions, while the Roman pantheon turned towards Italian gods, protectors of agriculture and trade.

After the middle of the 2nd century BC, the Greek gods and heroes became mixed with those of the Romans. This study will have achieved its purpose if it has succeeded in showing readers that this mixing was beneficial for both, and cannot be reduced to mere plagiarism and then destruction on the part of Rome of Greek religion, inventions, tales, legends and fables. Through its thinkers, scientists, mythologists, poets and philosophers – Cicero, Virgil and Ovid, to name only the most famous – Rome was able to make this ancient patrimony bear fruit. It became the indispensable agent of the Greek legacy, which it adorned without rendering it insipid, through the force of its own imagination.

Indeed, without Athens, the gods and heroes of the ancient world would not have existed. Without Rome, they would undoubtedly never have enjoyed the excellent popularization that has enabled them to pass through the centuries and come down to us.

BIBLIOGRAPHY

Primary Sources

Apollodorus of Athens, On the Gods
Cato the Elder, Treatise on Agriculture
Hesiod, Theogony, Works & Days
Homer, The Iliad, The Odyssey
Livy, Roman History
Macrobius, The Saturnalia
Ovid, The Metamorphoses
Servius, Commentary on Virgil
Tacitus, The Annals
Tibullus, Elegies
Virgil, The Aeneid

Secondary Sources

Cyril Bailey, The Legacy of Rome, The Clarendon Press, 1923.
Pierre Brunel,   Dictionnaire des mythes féminins, Le Rocher, 2002.
                    Le mythe de la métamorphose, Armand Colon, 1999.
Thomas Bulfinch, Greek and Roman Mythology, Dover, 2000.
Arthur Cotterell, Classical Mythology: the ancient myths and legends of Greece and Rome, Smithmark, 1999.
Ettore Pais, Ancient Legends of Roman History, translated by Mario E. Cosenaz, Swan Sonnenschein & Co., 1906.
Eric Flaum, with David Pandy, The Enclyclopedia of Mythology: gods, heroes, and legends of the Greeks and Romans, Courage Books, 1993.
Grand, Michael and John Hazel, Gods and Mortals in Classical Mythology, Merriam, 1973.
Grimal, Pierre, Dictionary of Classical Mythology, translated by A.R. Maxwell-Hyslop, Oxford University Press, 1986.
Richard Jenkyns, The Legacy of Rome: A New Appraisal, Oxford University Press, 1992.
Joël Schmidt, Dictionnaire de la mythologie grecque et romaine, Larousse, 1998.